THE JUDGMENT OF BABYLON

THE MYSTERY OF THE AGES

Roger King

BookLocker

Trenton, Georgia

THE MYSTERY OF THE AGES

THE RETURN OF JESUS CHRIST
DANIEL 8 & 12 UNSEALED

...ABORTION...

...FORNICATION...

THE JUDGMENT OF BABYLON

REVELATION 14:7&8

WW111

THE FALL OF AMERICA

ROGER KING

DANIEL CHAPTER 12

UNSEALED

THE
RETURN DATE

THE
GREATEST EVENT
IN HUMAN HISTORY

THE
"RETURN OF JESUS CHRIST"

THE DATE OF CHRIST'S RETURN
WEDNESDAY SEPTEMBER 15, 2027

"THE JUDGMENT OF BABYLON"

THE FALL OF AMERICA

THE REASON

FORNICATION
ABORTION

WHY THE FALL?

GOD'S JUDGMENT!

Dedication

To the memory of Irvin Baxter; End-Time ministries.

Epigraph

Daniel 12:4-9

The Lord said to Daniel

[4] But thou, O Daniel, shut up the words, and seal the book, even to the "time" of the end: many shall run to and fro, and knowledge shall be increased.

Daniel 12:5-9:

[5] Then I Daniel looked, and, behold, there stood other two, the one on this side of the bank of the river, and the other on that side of the bank of the river. [6] And one said to the man clothed in linen, which was upon the waters of the river, how long shall it be to the end of these wonders? [7] And I heard the man clothed in linen, which was upon the waters of the river, when he held up his right hand and his left hand unto heaven, and swear by him that liveth for ever that it shall be for a time, times, and an half; and when he shall have accomplished to scatter the power of the holy people, all these things shall be finished. [8] And I heard, but I understood not: then said I, O my Lord, what shall be the end of these things? [9] And he said, go thy way, Daniel: for the words are closed up and sealed till the "time of the end".

Revelation 14:6-9:

[6] And I saw **another angel** fly in the midst of heaven, having the everlasting gospel to preach unto them that dwell on the

earth, and to every nation, and kindred, and tongue, and people [7] Saying with a loud voice, Fear God, and give glory to him; for the hour of his judgment is come: and worship him that made heaven, and earth, and the sea, and the fountains of waters. [8] And there followed **another angel, saying, Babylon, Babylon is fallen**, is fallen, that great city, because she made all nations drink of the wine of the wrath of her fornication. [9] **And the third angel followed them**, saying with a loud voice, **if any man worship the beast** and his image, and receive his mark in his forehead, or in his hand [10] The same shall drink of the wine of the wrath of God, which is poured out without mixture into the cup of his indignation; and he shall be tormented with fire and brimstone in the presence of the holy angels, and in the presence of the Lamb:

Table of Contents

Forward

The Lord told Daniel to seal the words till the "time of the end". What did Daniel seal? And what did the Lord mean by "the time of the end?" Is there a path to the date of the RAPTURE, *Yes.*

This book is about unraveling the end-time scriptures found in the books of Daniel, Revelation, Matthew and II Thessalonians, and about where we are in Bible prophecy, how much time is left and most importantly, it is about scriptures that so many people have overlooked. The information in this book will take you on a tour of these prophecies and show you the timing of noted events that will happen in the last seven years. You will definitely be astounded as you read about the precise timing of events, including the rapture of the church, and America and her final days prior to the coming of Christ. This work took years to unravel but once you see how these scriptures fit together you will say, "Why didn't I see that?" These prophecies are telling you to be prepared for the coming war, the fall of America, and the date of the rapture. The fall of America and the rapture are forever linked, when America falls and is on her knees Jesus returns for Hs bride!

The above-mentioned event dates were sealed by God the Father 2500 years ago when He told Daniel to seal the words (Daniel 12:4,9) till the time of the end. These words have now been unsealed. God the Father also left a matrix of His perfect and completion number to prove that what was unsealed was of His authorship.

In this book the prophecies and story were started with the books of Daniel (12:6-8) and Revelation (14:6-12,) but you will see after reading all the connecting scriptures, that it could have been started from any of the four books mentioned above. The prophecies fit together like hand and glove. Amazing is the fact that these prophecies concerning America were written for the Bible by John the Revelator around the year AD 96; Daniel was written around 534 BC; Matthew was written AD 58-68, and II Thessalonians 2 was written by Paul around AD 54.

The information found in these pages proves these prophecies. They cannot be interpreted any other way. This Judgment will happen at the time stated in the prophecies. The information in this book proves this story and is available to all that really want to know the truth. If you really want to know the future you must study these scriptures. Daniel 11:33 says, "They that understand among the people shall instruct many." In the end-time be an instructor and you will be blessed beyond your knowledge!

This is a final warning! Daniel 12:4 says, "But thou O Daniel, shut up the words, and seal the book, even to the time of the end: many shall run to and fro, and knowledge shall be increased." Five verses later, he reiterates in Daniel 12:9, "And he said, go thy way, Daniel: for the words are closed up and sealed till the time of the end". This information also proves that God does exist, and that the Bible is correct and is the Word of God. We promise this book will astound you. If you are a Christian you need to know these prophecies and scriptures. The well-being of your family deserves as much. If you are a pastor you must know these prophecies and scriptures. Your congregations deserve to hear from you.

Floyd and Sue Searer

Introduction

The Judgment of Babylon-The Mystery of the Ages" was first placed in writing in the fifth century B.C. by Daniel the Prophet. Daniel at the age of 16 was taken into captivity by King Nebuchadnezzar and given the name of Belteshazzar. *Belteshazzar* meant "Bel Protect His Life" Daniels wisdom and divinely given interpretive abilities brought him into a position of prominence, especially in the courts of Nebuchadnezzar and Darius. He is one of the few well known Bible characters whom nothing negative is ever written. His life was characterized by faith, prayer, courage, consistency and lack of compromise. This greatly beloved man was mentioned three times by his sixth century B.C. contemporary Ezekiel as an example of righteousness.

The book of Daniel contains 12 chapters, chapter 11 alone contains over 100 specific prophecies of historical events that literally came true. Chapter 8 &12 have never till now been unsealed. God the Father told Daniel to seal the words in verse 4 and 9 till the time of the end. When God the Father had Daniel seal the words He also had Daniel seal the proof that once unsealed you would know without a doubt what was sealed was the work of "God the Father".

In Matthew 24:15 Jesus alluded to Daniel 9:27 when these words were penned; [15] When ye therefore shall see the abomination of desolation, spoken of by Daniel the prophet, stand in the holy place, (whoso readeth, let him understand :)

These words are meant for the Jews as this event happens after the Christians are removed in the rapture.

Now some 2500 years later Daniels writings are now completely understandable. Daniel 9:27 is a Matrix and basis for all of the "noted" days of chapter 12 of Daniel and chapter 11 of Revelation. As you read this book you will positively know that the days of Daniel 12 and Revelation 11 are the last 7 years of this age and is the timing element that leads to the date of the rapture and other listed events. For decades most if not all used the words spoken by Jesus in Matthew 24:36 without exploring when and to whom He was speaking; 36 but of that day and hour knoweth no man, no, not the angels of heaven, but my Father only. Jesus was clearly talking to the Disciples and at that period in time and up until Daniel 12 was unsealed no one did know.

Most think Jesus knew everything but clearly Jesus said He only knew what the father gave to Him. God the father authored the book of Daniel 500 years prior to the birth of Jesus, He instructed Daniel what to write and told Daniel to seal the words till the time of the end. It is important to note, He instructed Daniel to seal the words only till the time of the end. Not forever. It was odd to me that in all the years the key to unsealing the words was available, but no one thought to look in the Old Testament. Both Revelation 11 and Daniel 8 &12 had days listed for events to happen in the latter years. God's time clock was started but not complete. There were 3 days missing, the starting day which is 0 days, the day of WW111 which is 1,277.5 days and the day of the rapture which is 1277.5 days. Thus making 2 - 3.5 years or periods of time and as stated Times, time and ½ a time. Also making 1 Corinthians 15:52 complete at the last trump or at the end of the last 7 years. The key to solving this puzzle was in Daniel 9:27 and chapter 12 of Daniel and have been there for 2500 years. Time of the end meant time of the end clock, 365 days in the year.

The unsealing could not be accomplished until Israel became a nation and America was known as the world power. The last I looked days are time and all I've heard concerning the timing of the end time was Jesus said no man can know. This statement by all had been taken out of context and stated no one could ever know and was used so many times it became truth to all who did not want to look further for the truth.

We are in the last 6 years and Gods time clock is running.

The covenant or treaty, Abraham Accords is the treaty that turned all of the days mentioned into dates including the day of the RAPTURE of the church. This Treaty has been accepted by world leaders as a treaty between the Muslims and Jews. This treaty has been witnessed on **Thursday September 15, 2020** by world powers and by the Anti-Christ.

Chapter 1:
The Return of Jesus Christ

If I were to tell you that Jesus will be back on a certain date, what would you say? Well, you'd probably say **"no one can know the date"**, right? And I would say where did you get that from? And you would probably say Matthew 24:36, right? Where Jesus said only **my father in heaven knows the date, no not even the angels,** right? So far so good and I agree with 24:36 a very correct statement but you said, **no one can know the date**, right? Jesus never said **"no one could know"**, He said only His father knew. You then need to show me the verse in the bible where it says that **no one can know!** Can't do that can you as there is no verse in the bible that says **you can't know.**

What you are telling me then is that you are taking something that Jesus said and twisting it to something you have heard others say or taking it out of context, right? It's been taken out of context for 2000 years! What Jesus said when He was talking to the disciples was **that His father "only" knew the date** and **no one else knew the date "then"**, right? This statement by Jesus was made about 2000 years ago, was that prior to the Old Testament? No! Was that prior to the New Testament? Yes! Did Jesus in His earthly form author the Old Testament? No! Did Jesus ever say, I only know what the father gives to me? Yes! If Jesus knew everything He would have known the date, right? If I wanted to know what the father authored prior to Jesus where would I look? I would look in the **Old Testament**.

And where in the (OT) would I look? Well, I would start with the only chapter in the bible (OT) Daniel 12, this was written 500 years prior to Jesus and authored by the God the father, **Daniel 12:4 & 9 seal the words till "the time of the end". Do I now have your attention?** Why are words or days not listed in Daniel 12 vs. 4 & 9, and also empty in vs. 7-8 where it says times, time and ½ a time? However, spelled out in 11 and 12, and spelled out in Revelation 11:3 & 9. The Lord is telling you there is more that will be unsealed at "the time of the end". There had to be a reason for the days and somewhere there had to be a starting point! Wouldn't you agree? There is a starting point and that is part of what this book is all about. Daniel chapter 12 is God's last 7 year sealed time clock.

Now, if you can't possibly figure it out and many have tried, even the most learned Theologians have been unable to unseal chapter 12 of Daniel and what the Lord wants the Christians to know prior to His return. Everything unsealed and printed in this book is backed by God the father's perfect and completion number 7 and to my amazement how He covered America and the timing of His return is almost as awesome as the prophecy itself. He said seal the words till "the time of the end", He did not say seal the words "forever".

The good in this prophecy is God the father set the date of Jesus return 2500 years ago and the bad is that Babylon, *(America),* Babylon *(NYC),* that great city falls by way of judgment for fornication/abortion in the middle of the last 7 years and America is out of business by the time of the rapture 3.5 years later, in fact, the fall is one of the reason for the rapture. Babylon America, Babylon that great city is the one taken out of the way at times, time and ½ a time or 3.5 years into the 7 year tribulation and then the man of sin is revealed 2 Thessalonians 2:7-8. America wins this war but ultimately loses the battle. Much more in the book! And the reason for the fall of America? Well, you can read it yourself in Revelation 14:8. That great city falls in judgment due to **FORNICATION** which leads to *ABORTION!*

He placed the path to the date of Christ return only to be opened at "the time of the end." Had the date of His return been known it would have stymied daily salvation. Jesus did not know in His humanity nor was He made aware of the date of His return. God the father knew the Matthew 24:36 verse, only the father knows…would be carried on to all as "no one could know the time of His arrival". Thus setting up daily salvation. This was not a lie in any way but was taken out of context and truthfully speaking until Daniel 12 was unsealed was a true statement that only His father knew.

I have waited for many years to get this message out and am ever so humbled to bring this to you.

God the father knew that Matthew 24:36 would be taken out of context and it would eventually be stated to the public "that you could **never know** the day of his arrival. If this had not happened there would possibly be no immediate daily salvation. He always knew the date of His return and it was always in the bible to come forth at "the time of the end." By burying the date of return He turned salvation into a daily recommended requirement. If you die without salvation you are lost. People have a tendency to put off salvation wanting to postpone it and if the Lord could come back at any time you would have a tendency to seek salvation sooner than later. But the devil never quits! What a mighty awesome God we serve. God is so awesome in His mercy that no one should be left behind!

Now with the advent of knowing the date of His return, brings up another problem, **"those not saved"** prior to the last 7 years **"now knowing"** the date of Christs return may again want to wait till the last minute, ***"but wait"***, you now know the date of His return and if you are called and don't respond to Gods call you may be in serious trouble as this might be your last call, 2 Thessalonians 2:10 & 11 states, that you may be sent a strong delusion that you will believe the lie, What lie? The devils lies, there is no God, no salvation! You now know this so if you were not saved prior to the last 7 years, **"now is the time for salvation"** you dare not wait. A calling during this last 7 year period may be your last calling with the possibility of being sent a strong delusion to believe the lie if you don't answer the call. There will be no more callings.

If you will go to Chapter 12 of Daniel you will see 3 mentions of "days and also times, time and a ½ a time". You will also find time "in days" in Revelation 11. As opposed to what all have been saying for 2000 years "there is" timing in the bible and there is reasoning in this timing, "God the father" knew that in his "humanity" He would not know when He would return, thus He gave to Jesus only what He wanted Him to have, thus salvation **"is for the present not tomorrow"** as "Jesus could return at any time". Also the covering of America for the very reason that if He didn't cover America (America is the timing to the rapture and is found through the timing) everyone through the Ages would know when the end would come which also includes the day of His arrival. You will see this as you read this information verified through the bible and connecting it with "His proof" of authorship.

God the father knew that no one would believe this or other writings if He did not place "proof" this was His work and not mine. The message and proof of this is beyond our capability, want or need to do! Only He could accomplish this. See the Matrix, the Time Clock and the Incredible Sevens in the book for Proof of His authorship and not mine!

Every Christian knows that Jesus is coming to claim His own but are not aware of the actual date. 18 years ago when I started a search for America, I did not search for the timing of the rapture, only America, as I like everyone else just figured you could not know the exact date of His return. I looked at America in this way, **my God would not author a bible for all of humanity without including the greatest gospel preaching nation on earth, "how about yours"?**

An acquaintance of mine found the first mention of America in the book of Daniel 7:4 Independence Day. I have found 5 more prophecies or different writings about America since and they lead to a very unpleasant end time picture for America but a great future for the holy people, the Christians. Not only did I find America and the start date of WW111 and the reason for that war but also the date of the rapture!

Revelation 14:6-13 is an inline schedule of events as noted by Angel 1, 2 and 3 Judgment has come, Babylon *(America),* Babylon *(New York City)* that great city has fallen, do not worship the beast! At first glance this is just a bunch of words but in the "timing" and wording it's proven to be **(NYC)** and happening prior to the reign of the anti-Christ. There is no other great city that would equal **(NYC).** Our God is warning the Christians of this event, even giving us the date and time this will happen, and the starting date of WW111 and the participants.

I had been wrestling with **(NYC)** for a number of years and on January 22, 2019 (NYC) passed the **first abortion to birth bill** and I knew instantly why it was **(NYC).** There is no way around it. WW111 will start with the destruction of **(NYC)** on a given day, that date is **Friday March 15,2024 at noon.** Daniel 12:6-8, **"This is Gods Judgment on America" for fornication/abortion!** I am but a mere messenger believing there will be an exodus from this great city the likes that would make the exodus of the Hebrews from Egypt pale in comparison and will start the greatest crusade for Christ the world has ever seen. True believers will leave the city! Others most likely not!

WW111 starts the shattering of America's power (Daniel 12:6-8) and will be completely shattered by the time of the rapture 3.5 years later. Thus, the reason for the rapture of the saints, God will take His church home, hallelujah. At that point America is out of business so to speak. From this 9:27 treaty date of September 15, 2020 there is 3.5 years or time left to prepare for the timing of this horrible event the exodus of (NYC). There is much more to this in the following chapters of the book that will walk you through the bible with proof.

I take no measure for what God has placed before us, I am as dumbfounded as you will be once you have time to digest what is written here and I wish I were there right now to pray with you, assuredly you all are in my prayers daily!

If you're not saved by all means don't walk, run to the nearest alter, repent of your sins (you can repent in your home, car or wherever you are as long as you have a heartfelt repentance, receive Jesus, and turn from your old ways!) and then get baptized (most any Pentecostal church has facilities for baptism) in the name of Jesus Christ for the remission of sins and you will be ready to fly away to an eternity you cannot possibly imagine. God bless, see you on the other side!

"Now knowing" the date of Jesus return it would only be fitting that we should all be present outside waiting and praying for His return on that day and every day. It could even be a celebration of His coming and your last earthly meal with all of your friends. We need a welcome fit for the King of

Kings and Lord of Lords! Let's make that happen. There will be much more on this as time gets closer to the day of arrival! Jesus said I come as a thief in the night meaning His coming will be at the last trump, the end of the 7 years at midnight! That date again is **Wednesday September 15, 2027**. He will be a thief only to those that do not know Him.

You will find the proof of the date of His return in the chapters of this book, The Matrix and God's Time Clock and the Incredible 7's.

A short note on that day, I would love to see a mega search light at every Christian church shinning toward heaven in our nation or any nation to let Jesus know how much we love Him for what He has done for us. **"Light up America, for Jesus,"** might be the slogan.

On that final day of the rapture we Christians win big time!

Chapter 2:
Choosing The Right Path

Prophecy is about what is going to happen in the future. Why do I need to know the future? Well, of most importance it might help you choose the right path and prepare you for the tumultuous times to come.

What Daniel wrote 2500 years ago in chapter 12 of the book of Daniel is now coming true and the proof can be seen in the unsealing of Gods words to Daniel. You will be amazed at what was written that you could not see. The time-clock for all the end-time events was placed by Daniel, however the time-clock was in days not dates. By placing the timing in days the Lord sealed the words till the time of the end which meant there must be a key to unsealing of the balance of days, a place to start from and a way to change the days into dates. The covering of the last 7 years is precisely what the Lord did to insure no one would know when the end of the era would be until the time of the end was here. There always was a predetermined date for this age to end, the end of human government and the start of the millennial reign of Jesus Christ! That is mentioned in Daniel 8:19, and he said, Behold, **I will make thee know what shall be in the last end of the indignation: for at the "time appointed" the end shall be.**

Indignation; Strong displeasure at something considered unjust, offensive, insulting, or base; righteous anger.

SYNONYMS FOR INDIGNATION resentment, exasperation, wrath, ire, choler.

The indignation is what we're now going through. All the words penned in Daniel chapter 8 are meant for America and we have now gone through the most dishonest election ever, a reason for this indignation.

This story has been waiting to be told for 2500 years. We are in the last 6 years and we need to be prepared for the worst event (the fall of Babylon) and then the greatest event in human history, the return of Jesus Christ. After 20 years of studying the bible I am now more sure than ever that we must have the full armor of God in and on our presence at all times in these end times. So let's get to work and make sure you are ready for this event and the calamity that will be forthcoming. If you can understand all of this you will be used in a mighty way (Daniel 11:33) to instruct many that have been taught they would not be here when these things were happening.

This book is to warn all who will read and see the impending dangers we are facing and the time element thereof. If you do not comprehend this, you may be in a situation such as Katrina, the nuclear disaster and flooding of Japan or much worse. You and your family may be in harm's way in America and not be spiritually prepared for what you will be going through. The scriptures and dates placed in this book come straight from the bible. All scripture is from the King James or Amplified Bibles. I have not twisted scripture in any way. These very important scriptures mean exactly what they say, and say exactly what they mean, every jot and title has a meaning. The key to finding the meaning of these scriptures concerning America was placing the correct verses together. In each of the scriptures regarding the timing of these events and the Judgment of Babylon/The Fall of America, the timing is paramount to this understanding as you will see in the following pages. **You could not find America without the timing.**

When we pray at church for someone to be healed, we know that some are healed, and some are not, but normally we can't actually see that happen. However, in my studies of Bible prophecies, my faith has been made much stronger as a result of seeing Bible prophecies come true. You can go to Isaiah 53 and find the prophecies of Jesus' birth and the events that led him to the cross. These prophecies were written 1700 years prior to the events. In Matthew, Mark, Luke, Daniel, Psalms, II Thessalonians and Revelation, you will find what is actually going to happen in the next few years prior to His return and those prophecies were written some 2500 years ago even as far back as the book of Genesis. He told everyone in His word of His coming and He is telling us now of His return. Most missed His coming the first time! Are you going to miss His return this time? No, but are you going to be ready?

The Lord gave the inhabitants of earth 120 years while Noah was building the Ark to mend their wicked ways. Yet only eight souls made it through the flood. In Genesis 19:24 there are also the cities of Sodom and Gomorra that were destroyed by brimstone and fire. The very proof that these things actually happened, and the fact that the remains of Noah's Ark has been found along with the ruins of Sodom and Gomorra are there to testify of these facts. The judgment came because of unprecedented sin. I have been to both of the Sodom and Gomorra sites and embedded in the ash of the ruins are balls of sulfur and brimstone just as the Bible says. You will not find sulfur and brimstone anywhere else in that region.

The reason for the destruction of these cities is found in Romans1, Leviticus 18:22 and 20:13, and I Kings14:24, **fornication.**

Today and in our time the Lord has given us a 100 plus year warning with the start of the seven trumpets on 7/28/1914 with WW1 and this is the final warning as we are now in the last seven years prior to His return. With the amount of time left and what I have found in scripture concerning these last years I believe it to be a wake-up call. Somehow I believe Trump is going to lead us to the rapture of the church and is going to keep America from being annihilated in a coming war that most know nothing about. You can already see the signs of that war approaching. The prophecy of that war is in the book of Daniel chapter 12 verse 6-8 and Revelation 14:6-8. See the Matrix and Time Table and the Incredible 7's chapters of this book for the timing of events.

In my study of prophecies I found that pastors and prophecy gurus were not talking about America. I was told that America was not in the Bible. Well, an acquaintance of mine, discovered America in the Bible. "One verse"? I just couldn't believe there was only one verse about a country that God has so richly blessed. It was very hard for me to believe that God would not say something about a country that for so many years provided evangelist throughout the world. America, a country founded on Christian biblical principles and values, a country with so many monuments to God found throughout our land and in our nation's capital. Everyone knew that America was blessed of the Lord but not anymore the so called liberals think they are God.

My study patterns changed, I had to find the nation that God had blessed for so many years there had to be more. My research unlocked some very profound verses. These verses are in the books of Daniel, Revelation, Matthews and II Thessalonians. There are verses in Revelation 9 and Daniel 8 that depict a war that would have to include America due to the fact America could inflict that amount of damage. This war would also include a country that is capable of amassing an army of two hundred million men which is generally thought to be China but you will find in this book the role Iran plays. There had to be more! I needed more proof to insure what I was thinking was true. Everyone knows that in this nuclear age there will be another nuclear war at some point as there was in WWII. I'm not thrilled writing about this sad state of affairs but there is a need for you to know.

I had heard for many years prior to my studies that there was an evil one coming who would rule the world and we would be compelled to take his mark in order to buy, sell or even work, read Revelation chapter 13. This evil one would come in on a "Peace Platform" and would be so smooth, as to deceive, if possible, even the very elect the Christians, Matthew 24:24. This man was to come out of the final European Empire or the 10 horned beast. Everything I have read in the Bible states this and all the prophecy teachers I have studied also state this. So, if this is true, how does all of this happen? I can't tell you all the daily details but I can show you the prophecies that take us there. There is a law called Recommendation 666 in the European Union that gives the clue to who the Anti- Christ is and will be. He is the High Representative of the European Union his name is Joseph Burrell. More in chapter 10 on 666.

America has to be removed or in a vastly declining mode for the European Union to be in power at the end. There are too many prophecies pointing in that direction. However, I could not prove that until I found the answer to one prophecy Daniel 12:6-8.

This book is about how to recognize that event and other events that will happen in that seven year period. We are now in those last seven years. By negotiation of the Trump administration there is a treaty that the World Leaders along with the US and Israel have confirmed known as the Abraham Accords, a covenant for peace, Daniel 9:27 This treaty started the last seven years and will be broken three and one half years later with the Judgment of Babylon/the Fall of America. Then yet to come, will be Armageddon at the end of the seven years. This book is a guide to help you find this information in the Bible.

America is going to lose its power, but, if we turn back to God we may not be destroyed. The war that is coming will kill 1/3rd of mankind by fire, smoke and brimstone in a very short time as in Revelation 9:13-20. I pray you heed what I say. Jesus is coming back very soon. I wrote this to warn all who are interested and called to read this book that America is about to have many more serious problems than we face at the present and it would be a very good idea to be spiritually prepared, in tune with our creator, so to speak. I know that many will wonder how I could write this book, The Fall of America. I promise you, it was a bittersweet experience. In Revelation 10:9 Jesus told John to take the scroll and eat it and it will make his stomach bitter but his mouth as sweet as honey? In writing about the fall of my country, a country that I love and that so many have given their life for, a country that has been so good to me, makes this a really tough job to do, you want to stop the problem but there seems to be no way to make that happen. Its mind boggling to know what happens before it happens, but Jesus wanted us to know or He wouldn't have placed these scriptures in the bible. Remember, He said, I tell you these things prior to their happening so that when they do you will know that I am, who I say I am. My days are filled with the knowledge of what is coming and it is not pleasant to continually think about the devastation that is coming on mankind.

You also know from the conditions of the world today that America has chosen the wrong path by not honoring Gods commandments and it's just a matter of time before we implode and as of this writing the evidence is overwhelming that America morally is on the wrong track. The destruction that is coming will also happen to the opponents. God is judging the Christian nation first and the other nations will then be judged. This is a warning from God for all to be prepared. On the other hand I know what is at the end of the journey, Jesus is coming back to claim his own. I'm doing my best to be one of them. How about you? I trust and pray that as you read this book, and find that you need to know more basics in order to understand what is written here, that you will do as I did. My mother told me at the age of twelve when I saw these events unfolding I should get my bible out and read as if my life depended on it. In 1994 "I took her advice". Your eternal life does depend on it! Read your bible get to church, these events are close to culmination. You need to repent of your sins give your life to Jesus and be baptized in Jesus name for the remission of sin by full water immersion. If you do this, you will be ready for whatever comes your way. If you don't you may not be going where you really want to go.

Do you have children? Have you talked to them about Jesus? You don't have a lot of time left. As a responsible parent you should want your child to go to heaven so get with it! I've had and seen it take many years to finally see a friend accept the Lord!

I pray you and your family makes the right decision, choose Jesus.

It is your decision, be sure your right!

Blessed to be a blessing,

Roger King

Chapter 3:
The Signs of The Time and
The End of The Age

Matthew 24:3-14 now as He sat on the Mount of Olives, the disciples came to Him privately, saying, "Tell us, when will these things be? And what will be the sign of your coming, and of the end of the age? [4] And Jesus answered and said to them: "Take heed that no one deceives you. [5] For many will come in my name, saying, 'I am the Christ,' and will deceive many. [6] And you will hear of wars and rumors of wars. See that you are not troubled; for all these things must come to pass, but the end is not yet. [7] For nation will rise against nation, and kingdom against kingdom. And there will be famines, pestilences, and earthquakes in various places. [8] All these are the beginning of sorrows. [9] "Then they will deliver you up to tribulation and kill you, and **you will be hated by all nations for my name's sake.** [10] And then many will be offended, will betray one another, and will hate one another. [11] Then many false prophets will rise up and deceive many. [12] And because lawlessness will abound, the love of many will grow cold. [13] But he who endures to the end shall be saved. [14] And this gospel of the kingdom will be preached in all the world as a witness to all the nations, and then the end will come.

THE GREAT TRIBULATION
AT THE END OF THE 7 YEARS

<u>Matthew 24:15-28</u>[15] "Therefore when you see the 'abomination of desolation, 'spoken of by Daniel the prophet, standing in the holy place" (whoever reads, let him understand), [16] "then let those **(meaning this is for the Jews whoever reads)** who are in Judea flee to the mountains. [17] Let him who is on the housetop not go down to take anything out of his house. [18] And let him who is in the field not go back to get his clothes. [19] But woe to those who are pregnant and to those who are nursing babies in those days! [20] And pray that your flight may not be in winter or on the Sabbath. [21] For then there will be great tribulation, such as has not been since the beginning of the world until this time, no, nor ever shall be. [22] And unless those days were shortened, **no flesh would be saved; but for the elect's sake those days will be shortened.**[23] "Then if anyone says to you, 'Look, here is the Christ!' or 'There!' do not believe it. [24] For false Christs and false prophets will rise and show great signs and wonders to deceive, if possible, even the elect. [25] See, I have told you beforehand.[26] "Therefore if they say to you, 'Look, He is in the desert!' do not go out; or 'Look, He is in the inner rooms!' do not believe it. [27] For as the lightning comes from the east and flashes to the west, so also will the coming of the Son of Man be. [28] For wherever the carcass is, there the eagles will be gathered together.

THE COMING OF THE SON OF MAN

Matthew 24:29-31 "<u>Immediately after the tribulation of those days the sun will be darkened,</u> and the moon will not give its light; the stars will fall from heaven, and the powers of the heavens will be shaken. ³⁰ Then the sign of the Son of Man will appear in heaven, and then all the tribes of the earth will mourn, and they will see the Son of Man coming on the clouds of heaven with power and great glory. ³¹ <u>And He will send His angels with a great sound of a trumpet, and they will gather together His elect from the four winds, from one end of heaven to the other</u>.

THE PARABLE OF THE FIG TREE

Matthew 24:32-35 "Now learn this parable from the fig tree: <u>When its branch has already become tender and puts forth leaves, you know that summer is near.</u> ³³ So you also, when you see all these things, know that it is near—at the doors! ³⁴ Assuredly, I say to you, **this generation will by no means pass away till all these things take place.** ³⁵ Heaven and earth will pass away, but My words will by no means pass away.

The Fig tree being Israel, this is stating when Israel becomes a nation the generation that sees this happen shall not pass. The Lord will return in that generation. Israel became a nation on **May 14, 1948,** add to that **80** years for a generation this places His return at **May 14, 2028** or sooner.

The 2028 date was the only way to come close to the date of His arrival prior to unsealing Daniel chapter 12 leading us to the actual date of His arrival. Jesus said in Matthew 24:22 if the time was not shortened no flesh would be saved, 8 months shortened between Daniel 12 prophecy and Matthew 24 prophecy. Perfect words!

Chapter 4:
The Seven Trumpets

The book of Revelation is the only book in the bible that states if you read this chapter you will get a blessing. That's great, so why not read it a lot of times and get a lot of blessings. I did and I did get a lot of blessings. It's a case of the more you read it the more you understand it.

Most people have a hard time with the trumpets, there is a lot of camouflage in the verses to make you really study what is written to come to conclusion on what they actually are.

The first Trumpet on July 28, 2014 started with WW1. A lot of Christians think these trumpets have not happened. I can assure you all but one have already sounded. You need to know these trumpets to know where we are in the timing of events. If you can see that 1-5 and part of 6 of these trumpets have already sounded, the rest will be much easier to understand. The key in understanding these trumpets was to pick out something you could understand and run with it. God gave the inhibitors of Noah's day 120 years to stop their sinful ways. He has given us to date 100 plus years to get it right. It doesn't look to promising for a lot of people.

Revelation 8:1-6 Seventh Seal: Prelude to the Seven Trumpets

1. When He opened the seventh seal, there was silence in heaven for about half an hour. 2. And I saw the seven angels who stand before God, and to them were given seven

trumpets. 3. Then another angel having a golden censer came and stood at the altar. He was given much incense that he should offer it with the prayers of all the saints upon the golden altar which was before the throne. 4. And the smoke of the incense with the prayers of the saints ascended before God from the angel's hand. 5. Then the angel took the censer, filled it with fire from the altar, and threw it to the earth. And there were noises, thundering's, lightning's, and an earthquake. 6 So the seven angels who had the seven trumpets prepared themselves to sound.

TRUMPET 1 WWI Started on **July 28, 1914**

Revelation 8:7 the first angel sounded: And hail and fire followed, mingled with blood, and they were thrown to the earth. And a third of the trees were burned up, and all green grass was burned up. *Commentary: Revelation 8:7 I believe this to be WWI. However, there is nothing to judge this against. When wars were fought prior to WWII the army's would burn homes, crops and anything that could help accelerate the enemy's demise.*

TRUMPET 2 WWII started in 1939.

There is 25 years between WWI and WWII.

Revelation 8:8-9 then the second angel sounded: And something like a great mountain burning with fire was thrown into the sea, and a third of the sea became blood. 9 And a third of the living creatures in the sea died, and a third of the ships were destroyed. *Commentary: Revelation 8:8-9 this is WWII. There were 105,000 ships involved in WWII and about 36,000 were sunk, thus fulfilling the prophecy that 1/3 of the ships were sunk. Check it out at your library. The two atomic bombs were "like a great mountain" thrown into the sea.*

TRUMPET 3 Chernobyl happened on April 26, 1986.

There is 47 years between WWII and Chernobyl

Revelation 8:10-11 then the third angel sounded: And a great star fell from heaven, burning like a torch, and it fell on a third of the rivers and on the springs of water. 11 The name of the star is Wormwood. A third of the waters became wormwood, and many men died from the water, because it was made bitter. *Commentary: Revelation 8:10-11 this is the disaster at Chernobyl, in Russia. Chernobyl is the Ukrainian word for wormwood which is found in most Bibles. There is a lot of information available on this subject. The best is a video or DVD available on line by searching Chernobyl.*

TRUMPET 4

Revelation 8:12-13 then the fourth angel sounded: And a third of the sun was struck, a third of the moon, and a third of the stars, so that a third of them were darkened. A third of the day did not shine, and likewise the night. 13 And I looked, and I heard an angel flying through the midst of heaven, saying with a loud voice, "Woe, woe, woe to the inhabitants of the earth, because of the remaining blasts of the trumpet of the three angels who are about to sound! *Commentary: Revelation 8:12-13 perhaps the speeding up of time, Computer age, high speed internet. There is nothing to judge this against other than the fact that you can't seem to get enough done in a day.*

TRUMPET 5 the Gulf War started in 1990, a one year war. For America it was five months. There are four years between Chernobyl and the Gulf war.

Revelation 9:1-11 Then the fifth angel sounded: And I saw a star fallen from heaven to the earth. To him was given the key to the bottomless pit. 2 And he opened the bottomless pit, and smoke arose out of the pit like the smoke of a great furnace. So the sun and the air were darkened because of the smoke of the pit. 3 Then out of the smoke locusts came upon the earth. And to them was given power, as the scorpions of the earth have power. 4 They were commanded not to harm the grass of the earth, or any green thing, or any tree, but only those men who do not have the seal of God on their foreheads. 5 And they were not given authority to kill them, but to torment them for five months. Their torment was like the torment of a scorpion when it strikes a man. 6 In those days men will seek death and will not find it; they will desire to die, and death will flee from them.7 The shape of the locusts was like horses prepared for battle. On their heads were crowns of something like gold, and their faces were like the faces of men. 8 They had hair like women's hair, and their teeth were like lions' teeth. 9 And they had breastplates like breastplates of iron, and the sound of their wings was like the sound of chariots with many horses running into battle. 10 They had tails like scorpions, and there were stings in their tails. Their power was to hurt men five months. 11 And they had as king over them the angel of the bottomless pit, whose name in Hebrew is Abaddon, but in Greek he has the name Apollyon. 12 One woe is past. Behold, still two more woes are coming after these things. *Commentary: Revelation 9:1-11 The Gulf war. The name of the prince of the bottomless pit, in Hebrew is Abaddon, in Greek, Apollyon, in English, Destroyer, and in the Iraq language is Saddam. The smoke from the burning wells covered the whole land for a period of 3 months and was extinguished by an American company, one well at a time. If you will check out the length of the war you will find it took about 5 months to complete.*

TRUMPET 6 the four angels were loosed on September 11, 2001.

There is 11 years between the Gulf War and 911 attack.

Revelation 9:13-21 Then the sixth angel sounded: And I heard a voice from the four horns of the golden altar which is before God, 14 saying to the sixth angel who had the trumpet, "Release the four angels who are bound at the great river

31

Euphrates." 15 So the four angels, who had been prepared for the hour and day and month and year, were released to kill a third of mankind. 16 Now the number of the army of the horsemen was two hundred million; I heard the number of them. 17 And thus I saw the horses in the vision: those who sat on them had breastplates of fiery red, hyacinth blue, and sulfur yellow; and the heads of the horses were like the heads of lions; and out of their mouths came fire, smoke, and brimstone. 18 By these three plagues a third of mankind was killed—by the fire and the smoke and the brimstone which came out of their mouths. 19 For their power is in their mouth and in their tails; for their tails are like serpents, having heads; and with them they do harm. 20 But the rest of mankind, who were not killed by these plagues, did not repent of the works of their hands, that they should not worship demons, and idols of gold, silver, brass, stone, and wood, which can neither see nor hear nor walk. 21 And they did not repent of their murders or their sorceries or their sexual immorality or their thefts. *Commentary: Revelation 9:13-21 "Loose the four angels which are bound in the great river Euphrates. And the four angels were loosed, which were prepared for an hour, and a day, and a month, and a year, for to slay the third part of men." The 19 Demon Possessed Terrorists were in the four airplanes that caused the 9/11 tragedy and the perpetrators were from the Great Euphrates River area, they were loosed for a particular hour, day, month and year, to start the 6th trumpet blast and will lead to the war that will end the first 3½ year period of the seven weeks or seven years of the event as described in Daniel 9:27and Daniel 12:6-7.*

<u>Revelation 9:16</u> "They led an army of 200,000,000 men." China has boasted that it could field an army of that magnitude and the USA government fact book backs that up. China for the past several years has been making statements concerning Taiwan and its intentions to control that island, even if it must invade, and China is already making plans to do so. We now have once again North Korea flexing her mussles.

China has stated she could lose half of her population and still have a large country. You have to be blind not to see where this is going. China has stated she doesn't think we will trade LA, NY, or other major cities for Taiwan. The bible says it's going to happen. If you couple these problems with the North Korean, Taiwan, Iran problem and our financial instability you have a total nightmare. China also has a contract with Iran for the supply of oil and gas and has warned the USA not to interfere in Iran-China affairs. This war will happen 3½ years prior to Armageddon and will start the last 3 ½ years. The terrors will continue for Christians till the rapture of the church.

Revelation 9:17 says, "And the heads of the horses were <u>as the heads of lions</u>." Not the Lion but <u>as</u>. Daniel 7:4 states that "the Eagle (U.S. symbol) wings were plucked from the Lion (Great Britain) and made to stand on its feet as a man" (Uncle Sam). Does 7-4 ring a bell? (Independence Day) Contrary to what others say, the United States of America is in the Bible

TRUMPET 7 Rapture of the church.

If you have read all of the above hopefully you are convinced that we are in the six trumpet of time. If not convinced read it again and again. I've read most scriptures many times to come to a conclusion on what these verses mean. Sometimes you must overlook some items that make no sense at all and grab on to a verse that you can understand. There will always be a backup verse to prove your right. If you devote yourself to learning this you can place all the pieces of the puzzle together.

These trumpets along with the timing provided in Matthew 24:32-34 should convince you we are within a very few short years of the return of Jesus Christ. The maximum date for His return is 5/14/28 or 80 years past the date Israel became a nation. It can be sooner than that but not later.

Chapter 5:
America the Beginning!

Daniel 7:4: And the wings were plucked from the lion and made to stand on its feet as a man! *Interpretation: And the (eagle) wings (America) were plucked from the lion (Great Britain) and made to stand on its feet as a man (Uncle Sam)!*

Vision of the Four Great Beasts:

Daniel 7:1-8 "In the first year of Belshazzar king of Babylon, Daniel had a dream and visions of his head upon his bed: then he wrote the dream, and told the sum of the matters. [2] Daniel spake and said, I saw in my vision by night, and behold, the four winds of the heaven strove upon the great sea. [3] And four great beasts came up from the sea, diverse one from another. [4] The first was like a lion, and had eagle's wings: I beheld till the wings thereof were plucked, and it was lifted up from the earth and made stand upon the feet as a man, and a man's heart was given to it. *This is clearly America and Uncle Sam.*

[5] "And behold another beast, a second, like to a bear, and it raised up itself on one side, and it had three ribs in the mouth of it between the teeth of it: and they said thus unto it: 'Arise, devour much flesh!'

[6] "After this I beheld, and lo another, like a leopard, which had upon the back of it four wings of a fowl; the beast had also four heads, and dominion was given to it. [7] After this I saw in the night visions, and behold, a fourth beast, dreadful and

terrible, and strong exceedingly, and it had great iron teeth: it devoured and break in pieces, and stamped the residue with the feet of it: and it was diverse from all the beasts that were before it; and it had ten horns. [8] I considered the horns, and behold, there came up among them another little horn, before whom there were three of the first horns plucked up by the roots: and, behold, in this horn were eyes like the eyes of a man, and a mouth speaking great things."

How awesome is it that with all of the various writers of the Bible and even before America was founded, the date of our independence and the first mention of America was placed in the Bible for all to see. The chances of this happening are so incredible that I can't imagine the odds. But nothing is impossible with GOD!

If America Ever Ceases to Be Good

The words of Alexis De Tocqueville sound a deafening alarm:

"I sought for the key to the greatness and genius of America in her harbors; in her fertile fields and boundless forests; in her rich mines and vast world commerce; in her public-school system and institutions of learning. I sought for it in her democratic Congress and in her matchless Constitution. Not until I went into the churches of America and heard her pulpits flame with righteousness did I understand the secret of her genius and power. America is great because America is good, and if America ever ceases to be good, America will cease to be great." - (Alexis de Tocqueville - from <u>Democracy in America</u>)

Alexis de Tocqueville was a French statesman and philosopher who toured the United States with Gustave de Beaumont in the 1830's, observing America's culture and institutions. His two-volume work entitled <u>Democracy in America</u> paints a stunning picture of the greatness of our country through the eyes of two Europeans who had never experienced a true democratic republic. DeTocqueville's writings are filled to overflowing with references to America's morality and decidedly Christian basis as being the reason for her greatness.

These two Frenchmen knew, as did our founding fathers, that no government or social system can exist in perpetuity without the guide of moral restraint in the lives of the citizenry. They knew the truth of Proverbs 14:34, which states, "Righteousness exalts a nation: but sin is a reproach to any people." They saw in America a greatness which was the direct result of a people who believed in moral responsibility and righteous living; indeed, they saw an America that barely exists in 2010. De Tocqueville was correct in his assessment that America would cease to be great if she ceased to be good. When a nation decides to be free from religion as the U.S. has done, it brings upon itself consequences that were never imagined. It's a nice thought to believe that a society devoid of religious standards is one where all people are tolerant and everyone gets along just fine, but reality bites. Where there is no religious standard of moral conduct, every man is left to fend for himself, and every man then does what he thinks is best regardless of how it affects those around him. As morally bankrupt attitudes invade, and then pervade a society, the inevitable result is social, cultural, and political decay.

Can anyone cite an example in all of word history to the contrary? What de Tocqueville and Beaumont recognized is that our democracy was held together by the common belief among citizens that each one had the responsibility to live a life of **moral righteousness**. Such well-known religious principles as honesty, integrity, kindness, charity, and benevolence held together a melting pot of people from different lands and cultures. The common belief in individual liberty as well as the principles of decency, justice, and honor held together government institutions which believed their authority was given them by God.

And America was great. America was to the modern world what Solomon's Israel was to the ancient Middle East. Kings and princes came to our shores as the Queen of Sheba visited Jerusalem, only to depart in awe and wonder at the observation of God's extensive blessing upon our land. I do believe the finest days of our country are in its past, yet I also believe still finer days could be in our future if we returned to what made us great.

Can America survive if her foundational institutions of marriage, family, and community continue down the primrose path of destruction? Can a nation of ever increasing welfare rolls and government dependence ever regain the lost greatness of its "pull yourself up by the bootstraps" ancestors? Will a nation which condones perversion, **murder,** greed, **abortion,** moral relativism, and humanism exist for more than a few hundred years? No, no, and no.

This once great nation is faltering in her greatness because she is lacking in her goodness. We, as a society, have allowed a small minority of morally bankrupt individuals to set the national agenda since the turn of the 20th century. And now we find ourselves in a free-fall, ever spiraling downward to a most certain destruction. Friends, we MUST return to what's right and good on a personal level. We MUST demand a return to what's right and good on a local, state, and national level. We MUST return to what made us great or greatness will be forever lost in the wasteland of socialism and humanism.

I challenge you this very day to be honest with yourself; be honest about the condition of your own life as well as the nation as a whole. The first step to fixing the problem is admitting the problem exists. Look at your own commitment to goodness and righteousness; examine your own moral standards and ask from where they come; be willing to admit where you have fallen down and determine to bring an end to it. If you need help, seek out a Bible believing church where the truth of God's Word is the yardstick of moral measurement. You can never go wrong when you submit to the Divine Revelation.

The United States can indeed return to the place where Alexis de Tocqueville found her almost two hundred years ago. That is my sincere hope for the country I love; it is my sincere prayer daily. I don't know how long I have left in this life or how long our nation or world has remaining, but I want to be sure to leave a legacy of greatness to my kids and grandkids. So I will strive for goodness and righteousness as long as I live. Will you do your part?

Sources: <u>Democracy in America</u> by Alexis de Tocqueville

Commentary by: Matthew Gerwitz

What a great commentary by Matthew Gerwitz!

Chapter 6:
Is America In the Bible?

America, you're telling me that America is not in the bible? No way, my God would not leave out the greatest nation on earth! The line that America is not in the bible has been told to countless millions. I refused to believe that my God would leave out the greatest nation on earth, the nation that took the gospel of Jesus Christ to all of the world, the nation that has been so blessed by God for doing so. I positively refused to believe that America was not there and at this juncture in my life I am putting the final touches on my book on America, which turned out to be a book on the final chapter of America.

I have known for many years the bible alluded to Israel standing alone at Armageddon. My thoughts were if Israel stands alone what happened to America? Well, guess what, America is in the bible and it's defined by the timing of its fall. Yes, America does fall Daniel 12:6-8. I never had a problem believing what it was said you could never know the time of the arrival of Jesus Christ but America in the bible? I knew America had to be there. The most incredible story in this story is in finding America I found the path to the date of the rapture of the church. Amazingly the final fall of America and the rapture of the church are forever linked. The rapture takes place at the end when Americas fall is complete.

As you read this book you will find America was placed in the bible some 2500 years ago together with the date of the rapture of the church. Right now you are probably having hysterics as you probably have been told all of your life America is not in the bible and you cannot know the day of His arrival. Well hang on long enough to read this book and you will know more about the last 7 years than most prophecy experts. If you will take time right now and go to Daniel 12:4 & 9 you will see this, God the father is speaking to Daniel, and tells Daniel to seal the words till the "time" of the end. Today people are perplexed as they know bad things are happening on an unprecedented scale and nothing is being done to combat these sinful ways of behavior. What most don't know though is where we are on Gods time clock, we're close to the end of the age. I found the key to unsealing the 12th chapter of Daniel in 2004 but to find all the parts that are associated it has taken 16 years. There are 6 different scriptures that define or show the involvement of America. First, Daniel 7:4, then Daniel 8:5-8, 12:4 & 6-8, Revelation 14:6-13 & 9:17 and 2 Thessalonians 2:7-8. If you read these scriptures without reading this book you will say no-way but once all of these scriptures are tied together you will see how the Lord covered America and once you are able to see this you will say, I can't believe it's that easy to understand!.

The Trump administration has ushered in the start of the last 7 years starting with the Abraham Accords a 7 year agreement between the Muslims and Israel. This was zero day on Gods time clock and was the path to changing the days to dates, found in Daniel 12 and Revelation 11.

One of the greatest parts of this was finding the matrix of Daniel 9:27 and the perfect and completion numbers signifying this finding was authored by God Almighty Himself 2500 years ago. See the chapter on the Matrix.

If you have not received Jesus Christ as your savior I suggest you do so now. Don't wait, the day has arrived that the Lord can send a strong delusion that you will believe the lie that is currently happening before your eyes, there is no God! If you are called by God and fail to go it may be your last chance to accept Christ as your savior. 2 Thessalonians 2:10-11.

To see the proof and the way God the father covered America and the timing go to Chapter 9 God's Time Clock and the Incredible 7's. and God's Time Clock and the Matrix in Chapter 8.

I would also urge you to visit;

www.themysteryoftheages.com or www.thejudgmentofbabylon.com and view the 8 page article on 7's in the bible by; Michael Hoggard it will open your eyes to Gods perfect and completion number the number 7.

Chapter 7:
The Last 7 Years

THE ABRAHAM ACCORDS TREATY
DATE 9/15/21

The date of Christs return comes to light when you open Daniel chapter 12 along with the date of the start of WW111. The Abraham Accords treaty mentioned in Daniel 9:27 and dated September 15, 2020 is the treaty that started the final 7 years. The treaty is for 7 years due to the fact it is the final 7. The bible is never wrong and deducting the 7 year treaty from May 14, 2028, New Testament date, the treaty would have had to happen in 2020 or no later than May 14, 2021. We are now in the final 6.

Here's what I found, the Abraham accord was signed on September 15, 2020 and if you add 7 years of time as in Daniel 9:27 you get September 15, 2027 which is 8 months short of the date in the bible, New Testament. Perfect I said, as Jesus in Matthew 24:22 said if the time was not shortened no flesh would be saved. Perfect words! The bible is perfect! The time is shortened by approximately 8 months.

We also have the ending date of 2027, Gods completion number is 7 as you have seen in my book as proof of all I have written. 7 is completion. I expected it to end in seven which it did.

Seven years is not spelled out in the Abraham Accords treaty , however, this is the last 7 years to Christs return so the agreement will not be for more than 7 years and need not be spelled out, Daniel 9:27. This also needs not to be the confirmation of the covenant of Genesis 15:18 as most others studying prophecy thought, including myself.

Daniel 9:27 states he the Anti-Christ will witness the covenant or treaty "and that he has accomplished," you will find the path to whom the Anti-Christ is, spelled out in my book. In case you missed it his name is Josep Borrell, The High Representative of the European Union. He will be the one that is the recipient of the EU law Recommendation 666 giving him complete power in the event of an emergency.

Today September 15, 2021 is Yom Kippur day the holiest day in Judaism. A great day for the Lord to return on September 15, 2027.

There are a number of interpretations as to why Yom Kippur is deemed to be one of the happiest days of the year. My preferred explanation is that Yom Kippur is such a happy day because it is the day God forgives all their sins! Imagine the judge (or king, back in the day) pardoning you and letting you walk, notwithstanding all the crimes you've committed! You'd certainly be happy! And what a perfect day for the rapture of the church. The Daniel 9:27 agreement does not have to be between the Palestinians and Israel, the Abraham Accords is between the Arabs and Israel which includes all sects. Not just Palestinians.

When I started my quest to find America in the Bible, I had no idea what I was getting myself into. I not only found America in five places, but at the same time, uncovered the most valued prize of all, the path to the date of the rapture. The date of the rapture will be exactly seven years to the day from the treaty date. You will also find in this book the matrix of God's perfect and completion numbers, the number 7, that verifies all that is written here to be of God's authorship.

I originally thought Israel would gain this treaty by war. But it has happened through the art of negotiating, "The Art of the Deal," by President Donald Trump. In 2020 this agreement was finally completed. What an awesome God we serve. He knew the days involved 2500 years ago and knows that these last seven years will be very troublesome. **He wanted us to know these dates to enable us to carry on and complete any task He has given us.**

So many people have been taught that they would be raptured prior to the tribulation and that they would not have to deal with the adverse reality of the devil rearing his ugly head. Well, so much for their studies. Most pastors have had a distorted view of the last seven years, and it won't be easy to change their mindset, but try we must. Daniel 8:19 we are in the indignation now.

All pastors I have come into contact with, have one statement in their minds regarding understanding of the times. It's the statement Jesus made in Matthew 24:36: "But of that day and hour knoweth no man, no, not the angels of heaven, but my

Father only." They have failed to see that when Jesus said this, He was in His humanity and knew only what the Father gave Him. God the Father authored the Old Testament prior to the birth of Christ. I was quite surprised to find that no one had checked the Old Testament. In Daniel 12:4, 9, God told Daniel to seal the words to the time of the end and that is precisely what he did. The timing of the end-time events has always been there. The sealed missing words was the time, the days were missing in both verse 4 and 9 For further explanation on the time, go to Chapter·9, "The Time Table and The Incredible Sevens." All we had to do was turn the days to dates but there was much more to it as you will see in the following chapters.

Consider this;

You can have a ringside seat to the greatest events in human history , the return of Jesus.. To get on board, you must be a born-again baptized Christian. If you are not a Christian chances are you will not believe a word of this, so now is the time to start believing and also the time to get prepared. My advice, if you're not a Christian, is to start going to church and to get involved in church activities. Start studying the Bible and when called give your life to Christ; get baptized to get on board to fly away.

Chapter 8:
God's 7 Year "Time" Clock and Matrix

How incredible is it that God made it so that we would have to combine both the Old and New Testaments for a complete Bible and to complete the Matrix of Daniel 9:27. The Matrix encompasses the last seven years of time alluded to in the Bible, Daniel chapter 12 and Revelation 11 combine to form this Matrix.

The Old Testament book of Daniel was written 500 years prior to the birth of Christ and authored by God the Father. Jesus said in Matthew 24:36, when speaking of His return, "But of that day and hour knoweth no man, no not the angels of heaven, but my Father only." How correct!

The Matrix below, by God's Word, combines the Old and New Testaments together forever. In this Matrix you must use both the Old and New to unravel the timing of the final seven years of this Age. This is nothing short of amazing. God is warning America and the Christians, of the day and subsequent date, of the start of **WWIII** and the **RAPTURE**.

This is a word to the Jews to read both the Old and New Testaments.

THE MATRIX of DANIEL 9:27

Daniel 9:27AMPC: "And he shall enter into a strong and firm covenant with the many for one week [seven years]. And in the midst of the week he shall cause the sacrifice and offering to cease [for the remaining three and one-half years]: and upon the wing or pinnacle of abominations [shall come] one who makes desolate, until the full **determined end** is poured out on the desolator."

Daniel 9:27 is a synopsis of the final seven years. The beginning, where he (the anti-Christ) witnesses a covenant is equal to **"0 days"** on God's calendar of days for the final seven years.This doesn't mean he must be at the signing but on earth and alive and has seen the document.

In Daniel 12:4 and 9 God told Daniel to seal the book, seal the words, until the time of the end. What are the words that were sealed in Daniel 12:4 and 12:9?

Daniel 12:4 = **ONE THOUSAND TWO HUNDRED SEVENTY-SEVEN. FIVE DAYS:** This is in the midst of the week or 7 years where the anti-Christ causes the sacrifice and offering to cease.

Daniel 12:9 = **ONE THOUSAND TWO HUNDRED SEVENTY-SEVEN. FIVE DAYS:** At the end of the second three- and one-half year period, **THE RAPTURE OCCURS At the 7th or last trump! Jesus said I come as a thief in the night so it would be at midnight by reason of the timing. And as a thief to those that don't know him.**

The two verses above equal 2555 days or seven years of our time, the final seven years of this Age. At the end of the seventh year, the last trumpet sounds and the rapture of the church takes place, as referenced in I Corinthians 15:51-52: "Behold, I shew you a mystery; We shall not all sleep, but we shall all be changed, In a moment, in the twinkling of an eye, at the last trump: for the trumpet shall sound, and the dead shall be raised incorruptible, and we shall be changed."

Other words sealed in Daniel 12:6-7 are:

POWER = AMERICA and HOLY PEOPLE = CHRISTIANS

There are 7 scripture verses. The #7 is God's perfect and completion number and positive proof of God's authorship. I have stated many times that God would permit this to be completed only in His time, the time of the end, just as the prophecy says. I found the key to unsealing what Daniel had sealed, in the year 2004, but finding the rest of the story took years. God had it right to seal the words till the time of the end. We are now in the last six years. This is a warning to get your life in order and to be ready for the rapture. Put on the whole armor of God. If you think the anti-Christ element is bad now, just wait until WWIII. I guarantee you that you will need the whole armor of God to stand.

II Thessalonians 2:7-8 for the mystery of iniquity doeth already work, he who leteth, will let, **till he be taken out of the way, and then will that wicked one be revealed. This is NYC and the abortion law.**

America is letting this iniquity continue Revelation 14:7-8. Fornication which leads to abortion, and must be removed for scripture to be completed. America's fall and the rapture are forever linked. *Note regarding the complete fall of America: America will win this war (6th Trumpet War or WWIII) (Daniel 12:6-8; Daniel 8:5-8 Revelation 14:6-13; Revelation 9:13-18), but lose the battle. How can this be? How about Americas debt?

As noted in Chapter 5, America in the Bible, Revelation 14:6-13 describes Babylon *(America)* and Babylon that great city. Everyone knows who that great city is: ***New York City (NYC)***.

The prophecy in Daniel 12:6-8 states it will take three- and one-half years for the power of the holy people to be scattered. We are still in business after *(NYC)* is fallen, so to speak, but I can only assume that our debt will make it impossible to maintain our country. This shattered "completion" happens to be at the same time as the rapture, three- and one-half years after the war. Then Armageddon! What is the reason for the judgment? Again, Revelation 14:8 says that Babylon, Babylon that great city *(NYC)* is fallen because "she made all nations drink of the wine of the wrath of her fornication." **Fornication leads to ABORTION.** There was a law passed in New York City on January 22, 2019, that takes abortion all the way to birth! Thus sealing their fate. Jesus said, "Better to hang a millstone around your neck than to hurt my little ones!

From the bible and this book you "can now know" the date of these events. I don't expect you to believe me but open your eyes to what the bible is telling you. You must check this out! The information in this book will lead you through the bible with the above information and also through the most important section of the book **SALVATION.** I hope by and through my 20 years of devotion to finding this information that it leads you to a relationship with Jesus Christ. The way the truth and the life. I was no different than any non-Christian until I met Jesus and oh how my life changed. I hope yours does to!

THE MATRIX

Scripture	ch	vs.	Days	Dates

The Abraham Accord covenant September 15, 2020

He shall confirm a covenant with many for 7 years. He being the anti-Christ and High Representative of the European Union.

Daniel	9	:27	0 days to start the last 7.	9/15/20

The "Judgment" of Babylon that great city, New York City (NYC) falls do to fornication which leads to abortion, Revelation 14:7-8. On January 22, 2019 NYC passed the first abortion to birth law. God's judgment is carried out by Iran, Daniel 8:5-8. China enters, Revelation 9:13-18. America wins the war but loses to debt 3.5 years later.

Daniel	12	:4	1277.5 *TT&1/2 a time. WW111 @ noon	3/15/24

Start of the last 3.5 years.	0 (0 days of the final 3.5 years). The		3/15/24
anti-Christ has 3.5 years to rule, Revelation 13:4-5.			
At 1150 days the new Jewish temple will be re-cleansed, Daniel 8:14&26			5/11/27

Two Prophets killed in Israel after preaching 1260 days.

Revelation	11	:3	1260.0	8/29/27

Two Prophets are raised from the dead and on to heaven!

Revelation	11	:11	1263.5	9/2/27

RAPTURE of the church and complete fall of America!
At the last trump 7th year! 1 Corinthians 15:52.

Daniel	12	:9	1277.5 *TT&1/2 a time	9/15/27
Daniel	12	:11	1290.0 Gods wrath and ARMEGGEDON.	9/28/27
Daniel	12	:12	1335.0 Start of the new beginning.	11/12/27
PROOF	**79**	**77**	**7703.5** of AUTHORSHIP BY GOD.	

Chapter 9:
God's 7 Year Time Clock and The Incredible 7's

GOD THE FATHER TOLD DANIEL TO SEAL THE WORDS TILL THE TIME OF THE END.

Jesus said; I tell you these things before they happen so that when they do you will know that, I am, who I say, I am.

Most believe there are no provisions for the timing of events in the bible. This has been bred into us as so many have tried to place dates for various events only to see that day go by without any results.

Jesus said only my father knows the day and the hour, now stop and think about whom He was talking to and when, He was in Jerusalem talking to His disciples, this was clearly meant for them. In the Old Testament God the father told Daniel in chapter 12:4 and 9 to seal the words till the time of the end, what did Daniel seal?

Is there any scripture in the bible that states only my Father knows? YES! Matthew 24:36 Amplified Bible (AMP) [36] "But of that [exact] day and hour no one knows, not even the angels of heaven, nor the Son [in His humanity], but the Father alone.

Is there any scripture in the bible that says you "can't know the day? No! Is there any scripture in the bible where God the

Father said to seal up the words till the "time" of the end? Yes! Daniel chapter 12.

These words were only to be sealed till the "time" of the end! *Not forever!*

Daniel 12:4&9 ⁴but thou, O Daniel, shut up the words, and seal the book, even to the "time" of the end: many shall run to and fro, and knowledge shall be increased. ⁵Then I Daniel looked, and, behold, there stood other two, the one on this side of the bank of the river, and the other on that side of the bank of the river. ⁶And one said to the man clothed in linen, which was upon the waters of the river, how long shall it be to the end of these wonders? ⁷And I heard the man clothed in linen, which was upon the waters of the river, when he held up his right hand and his left hand unto heaven, and sware by him that liveth for ever that it shall be for a **"times, time, and half a time";** and when he shall have accomplished to scatter the **power** of the **holy people**, all these things shall be finished.

⁸And I heard, but I understood not: then said I, O my Lord, what shall be the end of these things? ⁹And he said, go thy way, Daniel: for the words are closed up and **sealed till the "time" of the end**. *Look at this closely, we all say end times. The clue in unsealing this is time, meaning the calendar.*

Also note, this timing is equal to the **7 YEAR MATRIX** of Daniel 9:27, seven years or times, time and ½ a time x 2 in days is equal to 2555 days. Multiply 365 days x 7 years and you get 2555 days divided by 2 = 2 equal 1277.5 days or periods of time. God the Father hid the timing in days. How incredible!

The missing words are; Power = America and Holy people = Christians

The Days missing words are; there are two periods of 1277.5 days.

ONE THOUSAND TWO HUNDRED SEVENTY SEVEN. FIVE DAYS

Daniel 9:27King James Version (KJV)

[27] And he shall confirm the covenant with many for one week *(7 years or 2555 days)* and in the midst of the week he shall cause the sacrifice and the oblation to cease, and for the overspreading of abominations he shall make it desolate, even until the consummation, and that determined shall be poured upon the desolate.

Matthew 24:36 KJV [36] But of that day and hour knoweth no man, no, not the angels of heaven, but my Father only. *The father placed the time in Daniel 12.*

Clue; He *placed days (for time) in Daniel 12 and Revelation 11. For what reason? To cover the timing so the generations would not be cognizant of the end time days or when the end would be. Our calendar is different than the calendar at the time Daniel was penned. The Lord knew someone (and probably who) would unlock these words at the "time" of the end, and at the time of the end. The days are now replaced with dates.*

There is no scripture in the bible that says you cannot know the day and hour when Jesus will return. It says only my

Father knows. Jesus did not say to not search or try to find the answer in fact He gave a clue in Matthew 24:15 alluding to Daniel 9:27 the key to the matrix. If you will notice in Daniel chapter 12 and Revelation 11 the timing is in days. The Fall of America in Daniel 12:6-8 is stated as times, time and ½ a time. The problem was to get times, time and ½ a time into days at the "time" of the end meaning our "time", our current calendar.

One of the most awesome parts of finding all of this is finding the mathematical proof that once downloaded properly it would show you that you were correct in your assessment. You can view this proof in chapter 9 **THE TIME CLOCK AND THE INCREDIBLE 7's.**

How awesome is our God? There is nothing I can say that would be justifiable to explain, proclaim, or mention His brilliance. God the Father authored these words to Daniel 2500 or so years ago and He has the day of His return to the "day" and "hour" in writing. Another clue on the timing is when Jesus said I come as a thief in the night, which will be at the 12th hour midnight or 7th trumpet in their respective time zones at the last trump. Scriptures say that in the blink of an eye we will all be raptured which means the live in Christ all go at one time it will not take hours or days. The bible states it will happen in the twinkling of an eye and all will be collected. People mock anyone that tries to find the date of Christs return. I said 20 years ago that someone would finally come up with the right timing and then no one would believe him. I had no idea I would be part of this miracle of miracles and am very humbled by it. Mocking someone without studying what they have to say only reflects on the one doing the mocking. Perhaps this information would cool their tongue if they would only read it.

Below was the only way to figure the time of the return prior to unsealing Daniel chapter 12. Keep in mind the return date here is a return of no later than May 14, 2028. However it can be earlier than that. Keep in mind also that Jesus said in Matthew 24:22 that the time would be shortened for the sake of the elect.

<u>Matthew 24:32 & 34</u> **(KJV)** "Now learn a parable of the fig tree (Israel); When his branch is yet tender (new), and putteth forth leaves (Israel became a nation in 1948), ye know that summer is nigh: Verily I say unto you, *This generation shall not pass till all these things be fulfilled*." When Jesus spoke these parables, He was in Jerusalem discussing the end time events with His disciples. Jesus used the fig tree in two ways. To explain: Branch is tender, or "new," and putteth forth leaves. **This is equal to Israel becoming a nation to explain to us these events.** He used the fig tree as in the Old Testament Hosea 9:10 and Jerimiah 24, "I saw your fathers as a first ripe in the fig tree at her first time," **pointing out Israel as the fig tree**.

<u>Luke 21: 29-30</u> "Behold the fig tree and all the trees; <u>When they now shoot forth</u>, ye see and know of your own selves that summer is now nigh at hand. "Again, Jesus was talking to His disciples and He was stating, Behold the fig tree (Israel) and all the trees (The Jewish People, His heritage); <u>When they now (Israel and the Jewish people) shoot forth (became a</u>

nation) "you yourselves" (the Jews) know that my return is at hand. Given the intense persecution the Jews have endured over the centuries they should be known as trees for enduring.

Matthew 24:34 Jesus said **"this generation shall not pass,"** Jesus is telling us something happened as a starting point on which to add the generation age to enable us to come to a conclusion on the timing of these events. Israel became a nation in 1948.

When reading Psalms 90:10 we find a generation to be 70 years but not more than 80 years so **the year 1948 plus 70 - 80** years is equal to the date that all these things will be fulfilled according to this scripture. The final date would then be from 2018-2028 that Jesus would return. Could the date of return be between 2018 and 2028 with the confirmation of the covenant being the catalyst that leads to the final 7 years and the final date and the rapture of the church? Yes, The confirmation of Daniel 9:27 must happen between 2014 and 2021. Why 2014? Because it didn't happen in 2013, so we must continue to watch for it to happen each year until 2021. The date of 2028 could end up being a lower date between the years of 2021 and 2028 considering the confirmation of the covenant must happen 7 years prior to His return. Matthew 24:32-34 states, **this generation shall not pass,** Psalm 90:10 states a generation is 70-80 years. Example; if the Confirmation of Covenant happens in 2016 the date of Christ's return will be 2023. Jesus said

We can know by Daniel 9:27 that the last "seven weeks" (seven years) begins with the confirmation of the covenant as in Daniel 9:27. If we can validate the signing of that covenant or treaty we should be able to come to a final year of the 7th trumpet sounding and the rapture of the church. The Fall of America will happen close to 3½ years after the confirmation of the covenant or it might be exactly 3½ years.

You have seen a lot of repeats on scriptures, this was done on purpose to help in your cross reference and perhaps lead you to a better understanding.

As you have read most of this book, I'm sure you have noticed a lot of timing days like 1260, 1263 ½, 1290, 1335 and so on.. I have not found where anyone that teaches prophecy has clued in on these numbers. They are overlooked and many say there is no timing of events in the Bible. I say they're overlooking some very important scriptures and timing. The Lord told Daniel to seal the scriptures.

Daniel 12:4 But thou, o'Daniel shut up the words, and seal the book, even to the time of the end: many shall run to and fro, and knowledge shall be increased.

The next three pages show a time charts. All the dates are straight from the Bible and the seven year time schedule is taken from our calendar. The Lord said seal it up till the "time" of the end so I was confident that he meant for us to place our calendar with these last seven years. Based on that. I was a little dumfounded when I divided the seven years 2555 days into two parts. I got 1277½ days, double 7's. I thought wow, how cool is that, but I had no idea what was about to unfold. When you view the incredible 7's page you will see why.

TMA 516 **"GOD'S TIME CLOCK AND THE INCREDIBLE 7'S"**

And when he shall have accomplished to scatter the power (America) of the holy people (Christians) all these things shall be finished. Daniel 12:7

ISRAEL BECOMES A NATION 5/14/1948

1948 Matthew 24:32 & 34 the generation that sees Israel become a nation shall see my return. This generation shall not pass till all these things are fulfilled. No later than 5/14/28

START OF THE LAST SEVEN YEARS DANIEL 9:27
The last seven year peace agreement

0 days **Date 9/15/20 Daniel 9:27** the Abraham Accords treaty

Rev 11:2 Temple to be constructed.

END OF THE FIRST 3 ½ YEARS / THE START OF WW111

Rev 14:7-8 **AMERICA'S "Babylon (NYC) that great city has fallen"**
2 Thessalonians 2:7-8 (NYC) removed from world scene...

Revelation 9:13-18 - 1/3 of mankind is killed.
1277.5 days **Date** 3/15/24 Daniel 12:6-8 scattering of "AMERICA's POWER"**
Daniel 9:27 Sacrifice stopped. Rev 14:9 do not worship the beast.

Daniel 11:31 Abomination placed.
Rev 14:13 Henceforth! Blessed are they that die in the Lord

0 days **Date** 3/15/24 START OF THE LAST 3 ½ YEARS**

Rev 14:12 Here is the patience of the saints, here are they, where? Still here on earth!
Rev 12:15-17 Jews deported and major Christian persecution starts.

Daniel 8:14-26 Temple cleansed at 1150 days.

1260 days **Date 8/29/27 Revelation 11:3** two prophets killed.
1263.5 days **Date 9/2/27 Revelation 11:11** Prophets raised.

1277.5 days **Date *9/15/27* RAPTURE OF THE CHURCH 7th TRUMPET!**

Revelation 14:14-16 Rapture of the church.

1 Corinthians 15:52 Rapture at the last trump.

Daniel 12:6-8 **"AMERICAS POWER" completely scattered.**

1290 days **Date 9/28/27 Daniel 12:11** The anti/Christ proclaims to be God.

Revelation. 14:17- 20 Wrath of God begins.

Ezekiel 38 **"ARMAGGEDON"**

Church returns with Christ for the battle of Armageddon..

A NEW WORLD

1335 days **Date 11/12/27 Daniel 12:12** blessed is he (Non-Christian) no mark. The Christians left 57½ days ago.

7703.5 days for a total, and double sevens to start the new millennium, consider this:

These dates are based on our calendar year. Seven years x 365 days = 2555 days divided by 2 = 1277½ days Each half ends in double sevens.

** Same date!

HMMM..., for the ending of events, such as the "Power of America Crushed" and the "Rapture of the Church." And double sevens start the new millennium.

Considering the start of the last seven years, we are now in the last 6.

GODS AMAZING PROOF

GOD'S COMPLETION AND PERFECT NUMBER

Endings: These dates end something: **"and end in seven"**

There are 17½ days between 1260 and 1277½

There are 27 days between 1263 and 1290

There are 57½ days between 1277½ and 1335

There are 127½ days between 1150 and 1277½

Beginning: These dates start the new beginning**: "and start in seven"**

There are 75 days between 1260 and 1335

There are 71½ days between 1263½ and 1335

Note; Scriptures ending in seven in the last seven years.

Dan 9:27	Abraham Accords treaty
Dan 12:7	WW111 & fall of NYC & Start of the fall of America
II Thessalonians 2:7&8	Fall of NYC
Rev12:15-17	Jews deported
Rev 11:7	Prophets killed
Rev 14:7	WW111 & fall of NYC
Rev 14:17-20	WRATH OF GOD and a total of seven

The MATRIX of Daniel 9:27 Note; seven major events at given times.

Daniel	9	:27	0 days	Abraham Accords treaty
Daniel	12	:4	1277 ½ days	Missing words = The start of the Fall of America
Revelation	11	:3	1260 days	2 Prophets killed
Revelation	11	:11	1263 ½ days	2 Prophets raised
Daniel	12	:9	1277 ½ days	Missing words= RAPTURE OF THE CHURCH
Daniel	12	:11	1290 days	The wrath of God A/C proclaims to be God
Daniel	12	:12	1335 days	A new beginning
	79	77	7703 ½ days	

Chapter totals- 79 Gods perfect and completion numbers- Verse totals = 77, Days total 7703.5

Counted, a total of 7 major events and a new start, beginning with double sevens.

Statement: The dates God had placed in the bible fit our calendar year perfectly and are witnessed by the incredible sevens. The above is proof of Gods perfect and completion number.

The above is proof of the Daniel 9:27 matrix with Gods perfect and completion number.

As a continuing effort to insure yourself that the above is true you will find how all of this fits with bible prophecies in the (TMA & TJOB book). There are a lot of people that say you cannot know when Jesus will return just from the statement Jesus made, only my father in heaven knows the day and hour. However, God the father has stated the timing to the day in Daniel12 and Revelation 11 and it is backed by His perfect and completion number. The book of Daniel was sealed with the last 7 years these events will happen. The Abraham Accords treaty with Israel was dated on 9/15/20 and shown above. The dates set by "God the father" are the exact days from the treaty signed by all parties including witness by the Anti/Christ. I hope this information has been helpful in your walk with Jesus. Do not believe preachers that say you cannot know the day. Jesus never said you could not know. God the father placed the timing in the 12ᵗʰ chapter of Daniel 550 years prior to the birth of Christ.

I personally wanted to know about America and the schedule of events and if you care at all for your family I would think you would want to know also. If you do not have a relationship with Jesus Christ I strongly suggest you get with it!

THE ABRAHAM ACCORDS TREATY AND THE PATH TO THE DATE OF THE RAPTURE

GOD has a word you, are you ready for His return? Have you repented of your sins? Have you been baptized by immersion in the wonderful name of Jesus Christ? If you haven't do not wait as the scriptures tell you that GOD will send you a strong delusion at a given time in the last days that you will believe the lie. 2 Thessalonians 2:9-11 we are now in the last 7 years, do not wait to do this! Get your ticket to this grand event with your heart felt repentance and baptism and fly away.

Matthew 24:32-34 King James Version (KJV) [32] Now learn a parable of the fig tree; When his branch is yet tender, and putteth forth leaves, ye know that summer is nigh:[33] So likewise ye, when ye shall see all these things, know that it is near, even at the doors.[34] Verily I say unto you, This generation shall not pass, till all these things be fulfilled.

Jeremiah 24:5Amplified Bible, Classic Edition (AMPC) [5] Thus says the Lord, the God of Israel: Like these good figs, so will I regard the captives of Judah whom I have sent out of this place into the land of the Chaldeans for their good.

Luke 21:29-30 King James Version (KJV) [29] And he spake to them a parable; Behold the fig tree, and all the trees; [30] When they now shoot forth, ye see and know of your own selves that summer is now nigh at hand.

Psalm 90:10Amplified Bible, Classic Edition (AMPC)[10] The days of our years are [a]threescore years and ten (seventy years)—or even, if by reason of strength, fourscore years (eighty years); yet is their pride [in additional years] only labor and sorrow, for it is soon gone, and we fly away.

Date of the Abrahams Accord treaty, Daniel 9:27

0 Days   **Date 9/15/20**

Daniel 9:27Amplified Bible, Classic Edition (AMPC)[27] And he shall enter into a strong *and* firm covenant with the many for one week [**seven years**]. And in the midst of the week [**seven years**] he shall cause the sacrifice and offering to cease [**for the remaining three and one-half years**]; and upon the wing *or* pinnacle of abominations [shall come] one who makes desolate, until the full determined end is poured out on the desolator.

Revelation 11Amplified Bible, Classic Edition (AMPC)11:1 A reed [as a measuring rod] was then given to me, [shaped] like a staff, and I was told: Rise up and measure the sanctuary of God and the altar [of incense], and [number] those who worship there.[2] But leave out of your measuring the court outside the sanctuary of God; omit that, for it is given over to the Gentiles (the nations), and they will trample the holy city underfoot for **42 months (three and one-half years)**.

Revelation 14:7-8Amplified Bible, Classic Edition (AMPC)[7] And he cried with a mighty voice, Revere God and give Him glory (honor and praise in worship), for the hour of His judgment has arrived. Fall down before Him; pay Him homage *and* adoration *and* worship Him Who created heaven and earth, the sea and the springs (fountains) of water.[8] Then another angel, a second, followed, declaring, Fallen, fallen is Babylon the great! She who made all nations drink of the [maddening] wine of her passionate unchastity [[a]idolatry].

2 Thessalonians 2:7-8Amplified Bible, Classic Edition (AMPC)[7] For the mystery of lawlessness (that hidden principle of rebellion against constituted authority) is already at work in the world, [but it is] restrained only until [a]he who restrains is taken out of the way.[8] And then the lawless one (the antichrist) will be revealed and the Lord Jesus will slay him with the breath of His mouth and bring him to an end by His appearing at His coming.

NYC REMOVED

1277.5 Days ** **   Date ** 3/15/24 Hour Noon

Daniel 12:6-8 Amplified Bible, Classic Edition (AMPC)[6] And one said to the man clothed in linen, who was above the waters of the river, How long shall it be to the end of these wonders?[7] And I heard the man clothed in linen, who was above the waters of the river, when he held up his right and his left hand toward the heavens and swore by Him Who lives forever that it shall be for a time, times, and a half a time *(or three and one-half years);* and when they have made an **end** of shattering *and* crushing the power of the holy people, all these things shall be finished.[8] And I heard, but I did not understand. Then I said, O my lord, what shall be the issue *and* final end of these things?

Daniel 8:5-8[5] and as I was considering, behold, an he goat *(America)* came from the west on the face of the whole earth, and touched not the ground: and the goat had a notable horn between his eyes, *(Israel).*

[6] And he came to the ram that had two horns *(IRAN),* which I had seen standing before the river, and ran unto him in the fury of his power.

[7] And I saw him come close unto the ram, and he was moved with choler *(irascibility; anger; wrath; irritability)* against him, and smote the ram *(IRAN),* and brake his two horns: and there was no power in the ram to stand before him, but he cast him down to the ground, and stamped upon him: and there was none *(CHINA Revelation 9:13-18)* that could deliver the ram out of his hand.

[8] Therefore the he goat waxed very great: and when he was strong, the great horn was broken; and for it came up four notable ones toward the four winds of heaven. *(The four horses of the apocalypse).*

Revelation 9:16-17Amplified Bible, Classic Edition (AMPC)[16] The number of their troops of cavalry was twice ten thousand times ten thousand (200,000,000); I heard what their number was.[17] And in [my] vision the horses and their riders appeared to me like this: the riders wore breastplates the color of fiery red and sapphire blue and sulphur (brimstone) yellow. **The heads of the horses looked like lions' heads,(** *America)* and from their mouths there poured fire and smoke and sulphur (brimstone).

Daniel Independence Day "America in the bible"

Daniel 7:4 Amplified Bible, Classic Edition (AMPC) [4] the first [the Babylonian empire under Nebuchadnezzar] **was like a lion and had eagle's wings.** I looked till the wings of it were plucked, and it was lifted up from the earth and made to stand upon two feet as a man, and a man's heart was given to it. *AMERICA* and *UNCLE SAM.*

Revelation 14:9-11Amplified Bible, Classic Edition (AMPC)[9] Then another angel, a third, followed them, saying with a mighty voice, Whoever pays homage to the beast and his statue and permits the [beast's] stamp (mark, inscription) to be put on his forehead or on his hand,[10] He too shall [have to] drink of the wine of God's indignation *and* wrath, poured undiluted into the cup of His anger; and he shall be tormented with fire and brimstone in the presence of the holy angels and in the presence of the Lamb.

Daniel 11:31Amplified Bible, Classic Edition (AMPC) [31] And armed forces of his shall appear [in the holy land] and they shall pollute the sanctuary, the [spiritual] stronghold, and shall take away the continual [daily burnt offering]; and they shall set up [in the sanctuary] the abomination that astonishes *and* makes desolate [probably an altar to a pagan god].

Revelation 14:13Amplified Bible, Classic Edition (AMPC)[13] Then I heard further [[a]perceiving the distinct words of] a voice from heaven, saying, Write this: Blessed (happy, [b]to be envied) are the dead from now on who die in the Lord! Yes, blessed (happy, [c]to be envied indeed), says the Spirit, [in] that they may rest from their labors, for their works (deeds) do follow (attend, accompany) them!

Revelation 14:12Amplified Bible, Classic Edition (AMPC)[12] Here [comes in a call for] the steadfastness of the saints [the patience, the endurance of the people of God], those who [habitually] keep God's commandments and [their] faith in Jesus.

Between the two 1277.5 days are events that happen at that time.

1277.5 Days **   are the same day & date. Date ** 3/15/24

0 days starting the last 3.5 years

Revelation 12:15-17Amplified Bible, Classic Edition (AMPC)[15] Then out of his mouth the serpent spouted forth water like a flood after the woman, that she might be carried off with the torrent.[16] But the earth came to the rescue of the woman, and the ground opened its mouth and swallowed up the stream of water which the dragon had spouted from his mouth.[17] So then the dragon was furious (enraged) at the woman, and he went away to wage war on the remainder of her descendants—[on those] who obey God's commandments and who have the testimony of Jesus *Christ* [and adhere to it and [a]bear witness to Him].

Daniel 8:14 Amplified Bible, Classic Edition (AMPC)[14] And he said to him *and* to me, For 2,300 evenings and mornings; then the sanctuary shall be cleansed *and* restored

1150 Days Cleansing of the Temple   Date 5/11/27

The Killing of the 2 Prophets

1260 Days   **Date 8/29/27**

Revelation 11:3 Amplified Bible, Classic Edition (AMPC)
[3] And I will grant the power of prophecy to my two witnesses for **1,260 days** dressed in sackcloth.

RAISED FROM THE DEAD

1263.5 Days   **Date 9/2/27**

Revelation 11:11Amplified Bible, Classic Edition (AMPC)
[11] but after **three and a half days**, by God's gift the breath of

life again entered into them, and they rose up on their feet, and great dread and terror fell on those who watched them.

THE RAPTURE OF THE CHURCH

1277.5 Days   **Date 9/15/27 Hour Midnight**

The 6ᵗʰ trump is over at midnight-thus starting the 7ᵗʰ trump at midnight!

1 Corinthians 15:52Amplified Bible, Classic Edition (AMPC) [52] In a moment, in the twinkling of an eye, at the [sound of the] last trumpet call. For a trumpet will sound, and the dead [in Christ] will be raised imperishable (free and immune from decay), and we shall be changed (transformed).

The anti-Christ proclaims to be God! GOD's wrath begins

1290 Days   **Date 9/28/27**

Daniel 12:11Amplified Bible, Classic Edition (AMPC)[11] And from the time that the continual burnt offering is taken away and the abomination that makes desolate is set up there shall be **1,290 days.**

THE NEW BEGINNING

1335 days   Date 11/12/27

Daniel 12:12Amplified Bible, Classic Edition (AMPC)
[12] Blessed, happy, fortunate, spiritually prosperous, *and* to be envied is he who waits expectantly *and* earnestly [who **endures without wavering beyond the period of tribulation**] and comes to the **1,335 days!**

7703.5 A new beginning starting in double sevens.

Total of Days not including the 1150 days for temple cleansing This is very important as these days will project and reflect Gods perfect and completion number. You can view this proof on the Time Chart and The Incredible SEVENS. At www.thejudgmentofbabylon.com

On the next 3 pages you will find Calendars for the years 2017 -2028.

The reason I placed these calendars is that you can count the days from the Abraham Accords Covenant or treaty date 9/15/20 to the exact day of the next event. As a Christian and from scripture you may know how horrific daily life might possibly be. You may be counting the days to your deliverance. Thus the calendars.

This will also help make you a part of showing someone else how true Gods word is and how in depth the Lord has gone to for you to understand what is happening.

Remember; You must be born again (having deeply repented of your sins) and baptized by full immersion in the name of Jesus Christ. You must not take the mark of the beast, which will be a chip implanted under your skin. Your repentance and baptism will get you a ticket to the greatest event in human history and you will fly away.

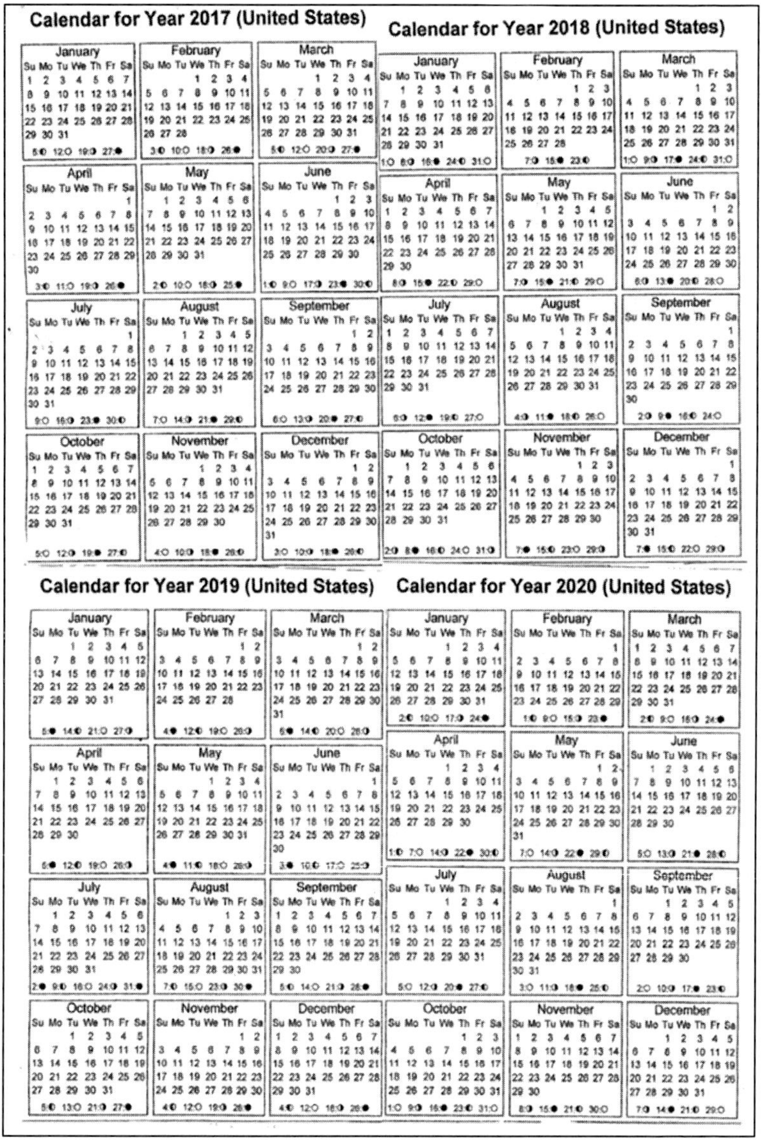

Calendar for Year 2017 (United States)

January
Su	Mo	Tu	We	Th	Fr	Sa
1	2	3	4	5	6	7
8	9	10	11	12	13	14
15	16	17	18	19	20	21
22	23	24	25	26	27	28
29	30	31				

5:○ 12:○ 19:○ 27:●

February
Su	Mo	Tu	We	Th	Fr	Sa
			1	2	3	4
5	6	7	8	9	10	11
12	13	14	15	16	17	18
19	20	21	22	23	24	25
26	27	28				

3:○ 10:○ 18:○ 26:●

March
Su	Mo	Tu	We	Th	Fr	Sa
			1	2	3	4
5	6	7	8	9	10	11
12	13	14	15	16	17	18
19	20	21	22	23	24	25
26	27	28	29	30	31	

5:○ 12:○ 20:○ 27:●

April
Su	Mo	Tu	We	Th	Fr	Sa
						1
2	3	4	5	6	7	8
9	10	11	12	13	14	15
16	17	18	19	20	21	22
23	24	25	26	27	28	29
30						

3:○ 11:○ 19:○ 26:●

May
Su	Mo	Tu	We	Th	Fr	Sa
	1	2	3	4	5	6
7	8	9	10	11	12	13
14	15	16	17	18	19	20
21	22	23	24	25	26	27
28	29	30	31			

2:○ 10:○ 18:○ 25:●

June
Su	Mo	Tu	We	Th	Fr	Sa
				1	2	3
4	5	6	7	8	9	10
11	12	13	14	15	16	17
18	19	20	21	22	23	24
25	26	27	28	29	30	

1:○ 9:○ 17:○ 23:● 30:○

July
Su	Mo	Tu	We	Th	Fr	Sa
						1
2	3	4	5	6	7	8
9	10	11	12	13	14	15
16	17	18	19	20	21	22
23	24	25	26	27	28	29
30	31					

9:○ 16:○ 23:● 30:○

August
Su	Mo	Tu	We	Th	Fr	Sa
		1	2	3	4	5
6	7	8	9	10	11	12
13	14	15	16	17	18	19
20	21	22	23	24	25	26
27	28	29	30	31		

7:○ 14:○ 21:● 29:○

September
Su	Mo	Tu	We	Th	Fr	Sa
					1	2
3	4	5	6	7	8	9
10	11	12	13	14	15	16
17	18	19	20	21	22	23
24	25	26	27	28	29	30

6:○ 13:○ 20:● 27:○

October
Su	Mo	Tu	We	Th	Fr	Sa
1	2	3	4	5	6	7
8	9	10	11	12	13	14
15	16	17	18	19	20	21
22	23	24	25	26	27	28
29	30	31				

5:○ 12:○ 19:● 27:○

November
Su	Mo	Tu	We	Th	Fr	Sa
			1	2	3	4
5	6	7	8	9	10	11
12	13	14	15	16	17	18
19	20	21	22	23	24	25
26	27	28	29	30		

4:○ 10:○ 18:● 26:○

December
Su	Mo	Tu	We	Th	Fr	Sa
					1	2
3	4	5	6	7	8	9
10	11	12	13	14	15	16
17	18	19	20	21	22	23
24	25	26	27	28	29	30
31						

3:○ 10:○ 18:● 26:○

Calendar for Year 2018 (United States)

January
Su	Mo	Tu	We	Th	Fr	Sa
	1	2	3	4	5	6
7	8	9	10	11	12	13
14	15	16	17	18	19	20
21	22	23	24	25	26	27
28	29	30	31			

1:○ 8:○ 16:● 24:○ 31:○

February
Su	Mo	Tu	We	Th	Fr	Sa
				1	2	3
4	5	6	7	8	9	10
11	12	13	14	15	16	17
18	19	20	21	22	23	24
25	26	27	28			

7:○ 15:● 23:○

March
Su	Mo	Tu	We	Th	Fr	Sa
				1	2	3
4	5	6	7	8	9	10
11	12	13	14	15	16	17
18	19	20	21	22	23	24
25	26	27	28	29	30	31

1:○ 9:○ 17:● 24:○ 31:○

April
Su	Mo	Tu	We	Th	Fr	Sa
1	2	3	4	5	6	7
8	9	10	11	12	13	14
15	16	17	18	19	20	21
22	23	24	25	26	27	28
29	30					

8:○ 15:○ 22:● 29:○

May
Su	Mo	Tu	We	Th	Fr	Sa
		1	2	3	4	5
6	7	8	9	10	11	12
13	14	15	16	17	18	19
20	21	22	23	24	25	26
27	28	29	30	31		

7:○ 15:○ 22:● 29:○

June
Su	Mo	Tu	We	Th	Fr	Sa
					1	2
3	4	5	6	7	8	9
10	11	12	13	14	15	16
17	18	19	20	21	22	23
24	25	26	27	28	29	30

6:○ 13:○ 20:● 28:○

July
Su	Mo	Tu	We	Th	Fr	Sa
1	2	3	4	5	6	7
8	9	10	11	12	13	14
15	16	17	18	19	20	21
22	23	24	25	26	27	28
29	30	31				

6:○ 12:○ 19:● 27:○

August
Su	Mo	Tu	We	Th	Fr	Sa
			1	2	3	4
5	6	7	8	9	10	11
12	13	14	15	16	17	18
19	20	21	22	23	24	25
26	27	28	29	30	31	

4:○ 11:○ 18:● 26:○

September
Su	Mo	Tu	We	Th	Fr	Sa
						1
2	3	4	5	6	7	8
9	10	11	12	13	14	15
16	17	18	19	20	21	22
23	24	25	26	27	28	29
30						

2:○ 9:○ 16:● 24:○

October
Su	Mo	Tu	We	Th	Fr	Sa
	1	2	3	4	5	6
7	8	9	10	11	12	13
14	15	16	17	18	19	20
21	22	23	24	25	26	27
28	29	30	31			

2:○ 8:○ 16:● 24:○ 31:○

November
Su	Mo	Tu	We	Th	Fr	Sa
				1	2	3
4	5	6	7	8	9	10
11	12	13	14	15	16	17
18	19	20	21	22	23	24
25	26	27	28	29	30	

7:○ 15:○ 23:● 29:○

December
Su	Mo	Tu	We	Th	Fr	Sa
						1
2	3	4	5	6	7	8
9	10	11	12	13	14	15
16	17	18	19	20	21	22
23	24	25	26	27	28	29
30	31					

7:○ 15:○ 22:● 29:○

Calendar for Year 2019 (United States)

January
Su	Mo	Tu	We	Th	Fr	Sa
		1	2	3	4	5
6	7	8	9	10	11	12
13	14	15	16	17	18	19
20	21	22	23	24	25	26
27	28	29	30	31		

5:● 14:○ 21:○ 27:○

February
Su	Mo	Tu	We	Th	Fr	Sa
					1	2
3	4	5	6	7	8	9
10	11	12	13	14	15	16
17	18	19	20	21	22	23
24	25	26	27	28		

4:● 12:○ 19:○ 26:○

March
Su	Mo	Tu	We	Th	Fr	Sa
					1	2
3	4	5	6	7	8	9
10	11	12	13	14	15	16
17	18	19	20	21	22	23
24	25	26	27	28	29	30
31						

6:● 14:○ 20:○ 28:○

April
Su	Mo	Tu	We	Th	Fr	Sa
	1	2	3	4	5	6
7	8	9	10	11	12	13
14	15	16	17	18	19	20
21	22	23	24	25	26	27
28	29	30				

5:● 12:○ 19:○ 26:○

May
Su	Mo	Tu	We	Th	Fr	Sa
			1	2	3	4
5	6	7	8	9	10	11
12	13	14	15	16	17	18
19	20	21	22	23	24	25
26	27	28	29	30	31	

4:● 11:○ 18:○ 26:○

June
Su	Mo	Tu	We	Th	Fr	Sa
						1
2	3	4	5	6	7	8
9	10	11	12	13	14	15
16	17	18	19	20	21	22
23	24	25	26	27	28	29
30						

3:● 10:○ 17:○ 25:○

July
Su	Mo	Tu	We	Th	Fr	Sa
	1	2	3	4	5	6
7	8	9	10	11	12	13
14	15	16	17	18	19	20
21	22	23	24	25	26	27
28	29	30	31			

2:● 9:○ 16:○ 24:○ 31:●

August
Su	Mo	Tu	We	Th	Fr	Sa
				1	2	3
4	5	6	7	8	9	10
11	12	13	14	15	16	17
18	19	20	21	22	23	24
25	26	27	28	29	30	31

7:○ 15:○ 23:○ 30:●

September
Su	Mo	Tu	We	Th	Fr	Sa
1	2	3	4	5	6	7
8	9	10	11	12	13	14
15	16	17	18	19	20	21
22	23	24	25	26	27	28
29	30					

5:○ 14:○ 21:○ 28:● |

October
Su	Mo	Tu	We	Th	Fr	Sa
		1	2	3	4	5
6	7	8	9	10	11	12
13	14	15	16	17	18	19
20	21	22	23	24	25	26
27	28	29	30	31		

5:○ 13:○ 21:○ 27:●

November
Su	Mo	Tu	We	Th	Fr	Sa
					1	2
3	4	5	6	7	8	9
10	11	12	13	14	15	16
17	18	19	20	21	22	23
24	25	26	27	28	29	30

4:○ 12:○ 19:○ 26:●

December
Su	Mo	Tu	We	Th	Fr	Sa
1	2	3	4	5	6	7
8	9	10	11	12	13	14
15	16	17	18	19	20	21
22	23	24	25	26	27	28
29	30	31				

4:○ 12:○ 18:○ 26:●

Calendar for Year 2020 (United States)

January
Su	Mo	Tu	We	Th	Fr	Sa
			1	2	3	4
5	6	7	8	9	10	11
12	13	14	15	16	17	18
19	20	21	22	23	24	25
26	27	28	29	30	31	

2:○ 10:○ 17:○ 24:●

February
Su	Mo	Tu	We	Th	Fr	Sa
						1
2	3	4	5	6	7	8
9	10	11	12	13	14	15
16	17	18	19	20	21	22
23	24	25	26	27	28	29

1:○ 9:○ 15:○ 23:●

March
Su	Mo	Tu	We	Th	Fr	Sa
1	2	3	4	5	6	7
8	9	10	11	12	13	14
15	16	17	18	19	20	21
22	23	24	25	26	27	28
29	30	31				

2:○ 9:○ 16:○ 24:●

April
Su	Mo	Tu	We	Th	Fr	Sa
			1	2	3	4
5	6	7	8	9	10	11
12	13	14	15	16	17	18
19	20	21	22	23	24	25
26	27	28	29	30		

1:○ 7:○ 14:○ 22:● 30:○

May
Su	Mo	Tu	We	Th	Fr	Sa
					1	2
3	4	5	6	7	8	9
10	11	12	13	14	15	16
17	18	19	20	21	22	23
24	25	26	27	28	29	30
31						

7:○ 14:○ 22:● 29:○

June
Su	Mo	Tu	We	Th	Fr	Sa
	1	2	3	4	5	6
7	8	9	10	11	12	13
14	15	16	17	18	19	20
21	22	23	24	25	26	27
28	29	30				

5:○ 13:○ 21:● 28:○

July
Su	Mo	Tu	We	Th	Fr	Sa
			1	2	3	4
5	6	7	8	9	10	11
12	13	14	15	16	17	18
19	20	21	22	23	24	25
26	27	28	29	30	31	

5:○ 12:○ 20:● 27:○

August
Su	Mo	Tu	We	Th	Fr	Sa
						1
2	3	4	5	6	7	8
9	10	11	12	13	14	15
16	17	18	19	20	21	22
23	24	25	26	27	28	29
30	31					

3:○ 11:○ 18:● 25:○

September
Su	Mo	Tu	We	Th	Fr	Sa
		1	2	3	4	5
6	7	8	9	10	11	12
13	14	15	16	17	18	19
20	21	22	23	24	25	26
27	28	29	30			

2:○ 10:○ 17:● 23:○

October
Su	Mo	Tu	We	Th	Fr	Sa
				1	2	3
4	5	6	7	8	9	10
11	12	13	14	15	16	17
18	19	20	21	22	23	24
25	26	27	28	29	30	31

1:○ 9:○ 16:● 23:○ 31:○

November
Su	Mo	Tu	We	Th	Fr	Sa
1	2	3	4	5	6	7
8	9	10	11	12	13	14
15	16	17	18	19	20	21
22	23	24	25	26	27	28
29	30					

8:○ 15:● 21:○ 30:○

December
Su	Mo	Tu	We	Th	Fr	Sa
		1	2	3	4	5
6	7	8	9	10	11	12
13	14	15	16	17	18	19
20	21	22	23	24	25	26
27	28	29	30	31		

7:○ 14:● 21:○ 29:○

Calendar for Year 2021 (United States)   Calendar for Year 2022 (United States)

Calendar for Year 2023 (United States)   Calendar for Year 2024 (United States)

Calendar for Year 2025 (United States)   Calendar for Year 2026 (United States)

Calendar for Year 2027 (United States)   Calendar for Year 2028 (United States)

Chapter 10:
His Number Is 666

THE TEMPLE AND THE ABOMINATION THAT MAKETH DESOLATE

The first Abomination of Desolation happens
in the middle of the 7 years.

Daniel 11:31 "And arms shall stand on his part, and they shall pollute the sanctuary of strength [*the temple*], and shall take away the daily sacrifice, and they shall place the abomination that maketh desolate." *What this is saying is they will place arms of the military of the 10 horned beast on the temple mount. **When? In the middle of the seven years.***

Daniel 9:27 "And he shall confirm the treaty with many for one week: and in the midst of the week [7 years] he shall cause the sacrifice and the oblation to cease, and for the overspreading of abominations he shall make it desolate, even until the consummation, and that determined shall be poured upon the desolate." ***When?*** *At the time they take away the sacrifices on the temple mount in Jerusalem. **In the middle of the seven years.***

The second Abomination of desolation happens
at the end of the 7 years.

Daniel 12:11 "And from the time that the daily sacrifice shall
be taken away, and the abomination that maketh desolate is set
up, there shall be **one thousand two hundred and ninety
days.**" *This is 1290 days into the second three- and one-half
years.*

This scripture is backed up by the following two verses:

Matthew 24:15 (KJV) "When ye therefore shall see the
ABOMINATION OF DESOLATION, spoken of by Daniel
the prophet, stand in the holy place, **(whoso- readeth let him
understand.)**" *This is meant for the Jews.*

Matthew 24:16 (KJV) "Then let them which be in Judea flee
into the mountains."

*There are two different abominations, one in Daniel 11:31, the
first abomination which is the 10-horned beast, and one in
Daniel 12:11, the second abomination. This second
abomination is the head of the ten-horned beast and is the
anti-christ. He will be the High Representative of the
European Union and this event happens 1290 days after the
sacrifice and oblation is halted in the middle of the seven
years. This second abomination happens after the rapture of
the church, 12½ days after the Christians are removed.*

These verses are for the Jews after the anti-christ proclaims to be God.

These next three verses are clearly meant for the Jews as this event does happen in Jerusalem and on the temple mount. *"Whoso readeth" is referring to the Jews that know they have missed the boat (rapture) so to speak.* They do not read the New Testament. They know that all of the Christians are gone and the ones that now realize that Jesus was their Messiah all along will turn to the New Testament for knowledge of what to do and what comes next.

II Thessalonians 2:4 "Who opposes and exalts himself above all that is called God, or that is worshipped; so that he sits as God in the temple of God, shewing himself that he is God."

Matthew 24:15 "When ye therefore shall see the abomination of desolation, spoken of by Daniel the prophet, stand in the holy place, **(whoso readeth let him understand:)**

Matthew 24:16 "Then let them which be in Judea flee into the mountains:"

Comment: *This is the time the Bible refers to as the time the Jews need to flee to the mountains. When? 1290 days after the middle of the seven years, after the fall of (NYC).*

His Number is 666

Who is he? Where is he? Is he in office? How will he receive his power?

HERE IS THE NUMBER THAT YOU HAVE HEARD ABOUT ALL YOUR LIFE.

(The Amplified Bible Classic is used for clarity.)

Revelation 13:18 (AMPC) "Here is [room for] discernment [a call for the wisdom of interpretation]. Let anyone who has intelligence [penetration and insight enough] calculate the number of the beast, for it is a human number [the number of a certain man]; his number is 666." Answer: **Recommendation 666** was a law in the Western European Union and was adopted by proxy into the European Union. **The law Recommendation 666 will give one man the power to convene the council of the European Union in the event of a worldwide emergency, thus making one man the recipient of the number 666.**

This is the number of the beast and the recipient of this number will be the beast. This law will give the holder of the office of the **HIGH REPRESENTATIVE** of the European Union dictatorial powers. **He will be the only person given this power through this law**. The person with the title High Representative of the European Union that has witnessed the Confirmation of the Covenant and the Fall of NYC) will be the beast of Revelation 13:18. The war of Revelation 9:15, 14:6-13, and Daniel 8:5-8 and12:6-8 will be the emergency that will open the door for this person to reign for forty-two months. (Below see Article 12 of the abridged notes for Recommendation 666 from the meeting held in the year 2000). This law is buried in the European Union's laws, much as our own laws contain hidden bombshells, as in the 2700 pages of Obama's Affordable Care Act. This law Recommendation 666 will be brought forward at the necessary time, which will be in the middle of the seven years.

This is Article 12 of the law Recommendation 666:

RECOMMENDATION 666 on the consequences of including certain functions of WEU in the European Union - reply to the annual report of the Council RECOMMENDS THAT THE COUNCIL: Article 12: Support proposals for the WEU Secretary-General and CFSP High Representative to preside over the PSC and civilian crisis-management machinery and give him <u>powers</u> to convene the Council of the European Union in the event of an <u>emergency</u>.

The war in Daniel 8:5-8 and Revelation 9:13-18, that takes one-third of mankind, would be a sufficient event to cause him to take power.

This is in keeping with Daniel 12:6-7, which starts the Scattering (KJV) of the power (USA) of God's holy people (Christians), or the Crushing (RSB) Rainbow study bible of that power and 3½ years of terror. America's "power" will be diminished or scattered in the middle of the seven years. This is confirmed in Revelation 14:6-13, the sequence of events with the three angels, stating, "Fallen, fallen is Babylon, Babylon that great city!" (AMPC) America will cease to have any power at all by the end of the seven years.

This also is in keeping with II Thessalonians 2:7, 8: "For the mystery of iniquity doth already work, only he who letteth, will let, *(speaking of fornication and abortion)* till he be taken out of the way and then shall that Wicked be revealed," to rule forty-two months. All who have taken the mark of the beast will be subject to the will of the anti-Christ.

There is nothing in the Bible that states his name must equal 666 in the sense of a mathematical value. I have downloaded Revelation 13:18 from 18 different Bibles and the letters of his name do not have to equal 666.

Merriam-Webster Dictionary definition of <u>Calculate</u>: to determine by mathematical processes; to reckon by exercise of practical judgment; to solve or probe the meaning of: FIGURE OUT.

<u>There are a lot of names that equal 666 but only one man will be the recipient of the law Recommendation 666.</u>

Have you ever wondered about this man? How will he come to power on a peace platform? After the scattering of America's power, all nations will be shouting Peace, Peace, and Peace! How will he deceive even the very elect were it possible!

The Bible clearly states that you will "**not recognize**" this man unless you are searching for him (Matthew 24:24), thus the deception. A word to the wise: If you read this information you can determine who that man is now. He is Josep Borrell to save you some time. The Pope at the time of this 7 year's will be the false prophet.

The Bible clearly states that he, the anti-Christ, will come from the last European Empire the 10 horned beast and will receive power after the Judgment of Babylon (The Fall of NYC). This is the event that triggers the start of the last 3½ years as I previously stated. The Judgment of Babylon and the war of Revelation 9:13-18 and Daniel 8:5-8, 12:6-7 and 2 Thessalonians 2:7-8 is in the time frame of the 6th trumpet. The events of 9/11 started the 6th trumpet, commencing on an hour, day, month and year. Revelation 9:15 states: "And the four angels were loosed, which were prepared for an hour, and a day, and a month, and a year, for to slay the third part of men." At the culmination of this war, one-third of mankind will have been slain. The anti-Christ will then find it easier to come in on a peace platform.

The European Union is the group of nations which the anti-Christ will rule, starting at the beginning of the final 3½ years, and for the last 3½ years he will be in total control. The Bible states that for you to buy or sell you will have to receive the mark of the beast.

According to Daniel 7:24 (KJV) three major powers (I believe they are Great Britain, France and Germany of the European

Union), will be subdued by law for this man to be in control. There are 27 Nations in the EU as of January 2020; the holder of the office of the **High Representative of the European Union** will be in control. If you will think of a picture of a wagon wheel, you will begin to see how the European Nations (EU) and this person's position fall in line with Bible prophecies. We have a circle with 27 nations as of January, 2020, and in the middle of that ring is the High Representative of the European Union.

He is in control of the various departments that perform the daily functions of the EU. He will be in control only after America's power is crushed. There is also another department that he controls it's called the military wing of the European Union or, as the Bible states, the ten-horned beast. This beast is the ten original nations of the Western European Union, which are today the large part of NATO. Let's place these ten nations in the middle of the circle between the High Representative of the European Union and the 27 nations. These ten nations are in the outer ring also. They are part of the 27; however, these nations are the Military Wing of the EU and will control the armies of the 27. The ten horned beast nations are Belgium, France, Germany, Greece, Italy, Luxembourg, Portugal, Spain, The Netherlands and the United Kingdom.

Your next question would be how one man gains control of the ten-horned beast and the 27 nations.

He gains control by law. Article 12 of Recommendation 666 passed into law in the year 2000. For access to these laws go to ask.com and look for information on European Union law Recommendation 666. You can also check out this link for information. http://curezone.org/forums/fm.asp?i=1118135

Chapter 11:
WW111 &, the Fall of America

DANIEL 12:6-8, REVELATION 9:13-18, 14:6-13
2 THESSALONIANS 2:7-8 AND DANIEL 8:5-8

Daniel 12:6-8 King James Version (KJV)

⁶ And one said to the man clothed in linen, which was upon the waters of the river, how long shall it be to the end of these wonders?

⁷ And I heard the man clothed in linen, which was upon the waters of the river, when he held up his right hand and his left hand unto heaven, and sware by him that liveth for ever that it shall be for a **time, times, and an half;** *(3.5 years)* and when he shall have accomplished *(meaning "something" happened and then an ongoing process)* to scatter the power *(America)* of the holy people *(Christians),* all these things shall be finished. *(This is telling you who it is! America.)*

⁸ And I heard, but I understood not: then said I, O my Lord, what shall be the end of these things?

Revelation 14:6-13 King James Version (KJV)

⁶ And I saw **another angel** fly in the midst of heaven, **having the everlasting gospel to preach** unto them that dwell on the earth, and to every nation, and kindred, and tongue, and people, *(America preaches the gospel).*

[7] Saying with a loud voice, Fear God, and give glory to him; for the **hour of his JUDGMENT is come:** and worship him that made heaven, and earth, and the sea, and the fountains of waters.

(Here is the "something" that happened from Daniel verse 7 above.)

[8] And there followed **another angel**, saying, Babylon *(NYC)* is fallen, is fallen, **that great city,** because she made all nations drink of the wine of the wrath of her fornication. *(Fornication leads to abortion and to date some 63 million babies have been aborted in America alone. NYC sealed its fate when they signed abortion to birth into law! China holds the prize at roughly 300m plus and will be judged severely). Part of the 1/3 of mankind lost to war.*

(Verse 9 proves the timing as the anti-Christ reigns for 3.5 years. Babylon that great city falls prior to the Anti- Christ taking control. This coupled with Daniel 12:6-8 when the power of the holy people is scattered there are 3.5 years left. This proves by the wording and the timing also to be America's great city. Remember these 3 angels are in sequence. Revelation 14:6-13 is a sequence of events).

[9] And the **third angel** followed them, saying with a loud voice, If any man worship the beast and his image, and receive his mark in his forehead, or in his hand, *(Revelation 13:5 the beast has 42 months to rule.)*

¹⁰ The same shall drink of the wine of the wrath of God, which is poured out without mixture into the cup of his indignation; and he shall be tormented with fire and brimstone in the presence of the holy angels, and in the presence of the Lamb:

¹¹ And the smoke of their torment ascendeth up for ever and ever: and they have no rest day nor night, who worship the beast and his image, and whosoever receiveth the mark of his name.

¹² Here is the patience of the saints**: here are they** *(Christians)* that keep the commandments of God, and the faith of Jesus. *(The Christians are still here in this sequence of events)*

¹³ And I heard a voice from heaven saying unto me, Write, Blessed are the dead which die in the Lord from henceforth: Yea, saith the Spirit that they may rest from their labours; and their works do follow them.

Revelation 9:13-19 King James Version (KJV)

¹³ And the sixth angel sounded, and I heard a voice from the four horns of the golden altar which is before God, *This 6th trumpet started with 911.*

¹⁴ Saying to the sixth angel which had the trumpet, Loose the four angels which are bound in the great river Euphrates. *(A Muslim oriented attack).*

¹⁵ And the four angels were loosed, which were prepared for an hour, and a day, and a month, and a year, for to slay the

third part of men. *(This is WW111 in the middle of the last 7 years and is the war of Revelation 9:13-18 and Daniel 12:6-8 and 8:5-8. New York City Babylon in this war is lost in Judgment on America Revelation 14:6-13.)*

¹⁶ And the number of the army of the horsemen were two hundred thousand, thousand: and I heard the number of them. *(This war will be perpetrated by Iran Daniel 8:5-8 and somehow they carry out Gods judgment on America by destroying New York City. Now let's see what the Lord authored to Daniel in chapter 8.)*

THE 2 HORNED RAM AND
THE HE GOAT WW111

The best way to explain this to you is through the wording of the Lord as it is complicated. Everything I placed, I placed in brackets so you could see the players.

Daniel 8 King James Version (KJV)

₁ In the third year of the reign of King Belshazzar a vision appeared unto me, even unto me Daniel, after that which appeared unto me at the first.

² And I saw in a vision; and it came to pass, when I saw, that I was at Shushan in the palace, which is in the province of Elam= *Persia= (Iran)*; and I saw in a vision, and I was by the river of Ulai.

³ Then I lifted up mine eyes, and saw, and, behold, there stood before the river a ram= *Media Persia = (Iran)* which had two horns: and the two horns were high; but one was higher than the other, and the higher came up last.

⁴ I saw the ram=*Persia Media = (Iran)* pushing westward, and northward, and southward; so that no beasts might stand before him, neither was there any that could deliver out of his hand; but he did according to his will, and became great.

⁵ And as I was considering, behold, an **he goat** = *(America)* came from the west on the face of the whole earth, and touched not the ground = *(Americas air power):* and the goat had a notable horn *(Israel)* between his eyes.

⁶ And he *(America)* came to the ram that had two horns **Media Persia = (Iran)**, which I had seen standing before the river, and ran unto him in the fury of his power.

⁷ And I saw "him" *(America uncle Sam Daniel 7:4)* come close unto the ram= *Media Persia = (Iran)*, and he was moved with choler irascibility*; (anger; wrath; irritability)* against him, and smote the ram= *Media Persia = (Iran)*, and brake his two horns: and there was no power in the ram= *Media Persia = (Iran)* to stand before him, but he cast him down to the ground, and stamped upon him: and there was "none" *(China Revelation 9:16-17)* that could deliver the ram= *Media Persia (Iran)* out of his hand.

⁸ Therefore the he goat (*America)* waxed very great: and when he was strong, the great horn was broken; and for it

came up four notable ones toward the four winds of heaven. *(The 4 horsemen of the Apocalypse.)*

This war will happen in the middle of the last 7 years Date, March 15, 2024

[9] And out of one of them *(Capitalism, Catholicism, Communism or Islam)* came forth a little horn= *(European Union)* which waxed exceeding great, toward the south, and toward the east, and toward the pleasant land. *(Israel &Armageddon 3.5 years later.)*

[10] And it waxed great, even to the host of heaven; and it cast down some of the host and of the stars to the ground, and stamped upon them.

[11] Yea, he *(European Union - Anti/Christ)* magnified himself even to the prince of the host, and by him *(the 10 horned beast)* the daily sacrifice was taken away, and the place of the sanctuary was cast down.

[12] And an host was given him against the daily sacrifice by reason of transgression, and it cast down the truth to the ground; *(Closed the Temple)* and it practiced, and prospered.

[13] Then I heard one saint speaking, and another saint said unto that certain saint which spake, How long shall be the vision concerning the daily sacrifice, and the transgression of desolation, to give both the sanctuary and the host to be trodden under foot?

¹⁴ And he said unto me, Unto two thousand and three hundred days; then shall the sanctuary be cleansed. *(vs. 26 clarifies this, 1150 days from the middle of the last 7 years.) See the Time Clock and the Incredible 7's.*

¹⁵ And it came to pass, when I, even I Daniel, had seen the vision, and sought for the meaning, then, behold, there stood before me as the appearance of a man.

¹⁶ And I heard a man's voice between the banks of Ulai, which called, and said, Gabriel, **make this man to understand the vision**.

¹⁷ So he came near where I stood: and when he came, I was afraid, and fell upon my face: but he said unto me, Understand, O son of man: for at "the time of the end" shall be the vision. *("Time of the end" same wording as Daniel 12, Daniel 8 could not be unsealed till Daniel 12 was unsealed. Amazing is the word of God. Chapter 8 was unsealed 16 years after the initial unsealing of chapter 12.)*

¹⁸ Now as he was speaking with me, I was in a deep sleep on my face toward the ground: but he touched me, and set me upright. ¹⁹ **And he said, Behold, I will make thee know what shall be in the last end of the indignation: for at the "time appointed, the end shall be".** *(The Lord knew exactly when the end would be and now, we know. He just didn't want anyone to know till an appointed "time"! The timing is everything in understanding these end time prophecies.) NOTE; Appointed time, 2500 years ago God had an appointed time for this age to close!)*

²⁰ The ram which thou sawest having two horns are the kings of Media and Persia.

²¹ And the rough goat is the king of Grecia: and the great horn that is between his eyes is the first king.

²² Now that being broken, whereas four stood up for it, four kingdoms shall stand up out of the nation, but not in his power.

²³ And in the latter time of their kingdom, when the transgressors are come to the full, a king of fierce countenance *(Anti/Christ),* and understanding dark sentences, shall stand up.

²⁴ And his power *(Law Recommendation 666)* shall be mighty but not by his own power, *(European Union)*: and he shall destroy wonderfully, and shall prosper, and practise, and shall destroy the mighty and the holy people. *(This law gives one man the power to convene the council of the European Union in the event of an emergency thus giving him dictatorial power!)*

²⁵ And through his policy also he shall cause craft to prosper in his hand; and he shall magnify himself in his heart, and by peace shall destroy many: he shall also stand up against the Prince of princes; but he *(Anti/Christ)* shall be broken without hand.

²⁶ And the vision of the **evening and the morning** which was told is true: wherefore shut thou up the vision; for it shall be for many days. *(2300 divided by 2 = 1150 days.)*

²⁷ And I Daniel fainted, and was sick certain days; afterward I rose up, and did the king's business; and I was astonished at the vision, but none understood it.

(What an awesome prophecy, there is no one like our God! All of this was placed 2500 years ago, 500 years prior to Jesus being born. I looked at this Daniel 8 in 2004 when I received the key to unsealing Daniel 12 but I thought who can understand this? This information has come to me by continually counting on the Lord to show me what He is saying and trying to find what you could not see. I took another look at Daniel 8 after Daniel 12 was completely understood and walked right through it. Thank you Jesus! How perfect are your words.)

Back to Revelation 9:17

¹⁷ And thus I saw the horses in the vision, and them that sat on them, having breastplates of fire, and of jacinth, and brimstone: **and the heads of the horses were as the heads of lions**; *(America)* and out of their mouths issued fire and smoke and brimstone.

(Symbols for major end time player countries are as follows: America is the Eagle, England is the Lion, Russia is the Bear and Germany is the Leopard. <u>Daniel 7:4 The eagle wings were plucked from the lion and made to stand on the</u>

<u>feet as a man.</u> ***This is indicating in Bible Prophecy that "America" was born of the Lion (England) and then made to stand by herself as a man (Uncle Sam).***

Revelation 9:17. The heads of the horses were as the heads of lions. *(If you are sitting on the horse, who is the head of the horse? You of course and you are, "as the heads of Lions." This verse is also another proof of divine intervention in the writing of the Bible. What are the odds that Daniel 7:4 would show up as Independence Day? Or that we would be as the heads of lions?)*

(In reading Daniel 7:4 you find, and the eagle wings (America) were plucked from the lion (Great Britain) and made to stand on its feet as a man, (Uncle Sam).

[18] By these three was the third part of men killed, by the fire, and by the smoke, and by the brimstone, which issued out of their mouths.

Revelation 9:19-18 for their power is in their mouth and in their tails; for their tails are like serpents, having heads; and with them they do harm. [20] But the rest of mankind, who were not killed by these plagues, did not repent of the works of their hands, that they should not worship demons, and idols of gold, silver, brass, stone, and wood, which can neither see nor hear nor walk. [21] And they did not repent of their **murders or their sorceries or their sexual immorality or their thefts.**

(The above verses from Revelation 9:15-18 indicate a horrible war coming on America (remember this Judgment is on Babylon (America).

2 Thessalonians *2:7-8* [7] for the mystery of iniquity doth already work: only he who now letteth will let, until he be taken out of the way. *(NYC) will be taken in judgment on America, Revelation 14:8, for fornication which leads to abortion and America will fall completely (30 trillion debt) by the time of the rapture.)*

(The above events happen as they are written in the bible. Prophecy must come forth as written. Armageddon will follow this war 3.5 years later just 12.5 days after the rapture.)

(I apologize for all of the similar verses used so many times in this book but I used them to clarify the scriptures and get the point across.)

Why would the Lord warn America of the date of WW111? It looks by what is written there are 3 players in this war America, Iran and China and by judging America first judgment will come on Iran and China. Thus starting the apocalypse as stated in Daniel 8.

Chapter 12:
The Killing of The Two Prophets

Jews Deported
Israel's Protection

Revelation 11:1-19 And there was given me a <u>reed</u> like unto a rod: and the angel stood, saying, Rise, and measure the temple of God, and the altar, and them that <u>worship</u> therein. *The temple was re-cleansed at 1150 days after the sacrifice and oblation was stopped in the middle of the seven years and is now once again being worshiped in. This is 110 days prior to the two witnesses being killed and 127½ days prior to the rapture of the church. This verse also tells you that there is a new temple on the temple mount.*

² But the <u>court</u> which is without the <u>temple</u> leave out, and measure it not; for it is given unto the Gentiles: and the <u>holy city</u> shall they tread under foot **forty and two months 1,277½ days into the second half of the 7 years.** *This verse is stating that the Gentiles will be using the temple mount till the rapture of the church at 1277 ½ days or the 7th trump or the 7th year.*

³ And I will give power unto my two <u>witnesses</u>, and they <u>shall prophesy a thousand two hundred and threescore days,</u> *(1260 days)* clothed in sackcloth. ⁴ These are the two <u>olive trees</u>, and the two candlesticks standing before the God of the earth.

⁵ And if any man will hurt them, fire proceedeth out of their mouth, and devoureth their enemies: and if any man will hurt

them, he must in this manner be killed. [6] These have power to shut heaven that it rain not in the days of their prophecy: and have power over waters to turn them to blood, and to smite the earth with all plagues, as often as they will. [7] And when they shall have finished their testimony, the beast that ascendeth out of the bottomless pit shall make war against them, and shall overcome them, and kill them. [8] And their dead bodies shall lie in the street of the great city, which spiritually is called Sodom and Egypt, where also our Lord was crucified.

[9] And they of the people and kindreds and tongues and nations shall see their dead bodies three days and an half, and shall not suffer their dead bodies to be put in graves. [10] And they that dwell upon the earth shall rejoice over them, and make merry, and shall send gifts one to another; because these two prophets tormented them that dwelt on the earth.

[11] And after three days and an half the spirit of life from God entered into them, and they stood upon their feet; and great fear fell upon them which saw them. [12] And they heard a great voice from heaven saying unto them, Come up hither. And they ascended up to heaven in a cloud; and their enemies beheld them. [13] And the same hour was there a great earthquake, and the tenth part of the city fell, and in the earthquake were slain of men seven thousand: and the remnant were affrighted, and gave glory to the God of heaven. [14] The second woe is past; and, behold, the third woe cometh quickly.

[15] And the seventh angel sounded; and there were great voices in heaven, saying, The kingdoms of this world are become the

kingdoms of our Lord, and of his Christ; and he shall reign for ever and ever. [16] And the four and twenty elders, which sat before God on their seats, fell upon their faces, and worshipped God, [17] Saying, We give thee thanks, O LORD God Almighty, which art, and wast, and art to come; because thou hast taken to thee thy great power, and hast reigned. [18] And the nations were angry, <u>and thy wrath is come,</u> and the time of the dead, that they should be judged, and that thou shouldest give reward unto thy servants the prophets, and to the saints, and them that fear thy name, small and great; and shouldest destroy them which destroy the earth. [19] And the temple of God was opened in heaven, and there was seen in his temple the ark of his testament: and there were lightnings, and voices, and thundering's, and an earthquake, and great hail. ***There is sure to be a TV camera trained on these two prophets for MOST of the 1263 ½ days.***

THE JEWS WILL BE EXPELLED FROM THE EUROPEAN UNION
Or Any Country Under the Control of The Anti-Christ

Revelation 12:15-17 So the serpent spewed out of his mouth water like a flood after the woman, that he might cause her to be carried away by the flood. 16 But the earth helped the woman, and the earth opened its mouth and swallowed up the flood which the dragon had spewed out of his mouth. 17 And the dragon was enraged with the woman, and he went to make war with the rest of her offspring, who keep the commandments of God and have the testimony of Jesus Christ.

What does Revelation 12:15-17 mean? As you read these verses again, note the additions to help you understand exactly what the Bible was trying to convey.

Interpretation;

Revelation 12:15 (KJV) "And the serpent *(anti-Christ)* cast out of his mouth water *(Jews)* as a flood after the woman *(Israel)* that he might cause her to be carried away of the flood." (Cause: Israel great financial and population problems).

Revelation 12:16 (KJV) "And the earth *(Christians)* helped the woman *(Israel)* and the earth *(Christians)* opened her mouth, and swallowed up the flood *(Jews)* which the dragon *(anti-Christ)* cast out of his mouth."

Revelation 12:17 (KJV) "And the dragon *(anti-Christ)* was wroth with the woman *(Israel),* and went to make war with the remnant of her seed *(Christians)*, which keep the commandments of God and have the testimony of Jesus Christ."

My Comments: Revelation 12: 15-17 The anti-Christ is going to expel the Jews from the European Union or any other country he controls and when that fails to accomplish what he intends, he will make war with the Christians as the Bible says, the Christians will be greatly persecuted. At the present time persecution is getting more severe in Islamic countries. The antichrist will deceive all who do not have the witness of Jesus Christ. Persecution of the Christians is currently on a level we've never seen since WW11.

There may be some of you who remember that Germany prior to the start of WW II expelled the Jews. That didn't work. Then there was the aftermath. Most Jews today do not believe that Jesus is their Messiah. There is a group called The Temple Mount Faithful who are of this persuasion and they will start the 2000 year old ancient practice of animal sacrifice. According to Revelation 11:1-2, a temple must be built prior to the power *(USA)* of the holy people *(Christians)* being crushed. In fact this temple must be built prior to the start of the last three and one half years for the anti-Christ to stop the sacrifice in Daniel 9:27. There must be a Temple in which to place the abomination that makes desolate as in Daniel 11:31.

Daniel 9:27 (RSB) "This king will make a seven-year treaty with the people, but after half that time *(3½ years)*, he will break his pledge and stop the Jews from their sacrifices and their offerings. Daniel 12:11 then as a climax *(1290 days later at the end of the seven years)* to all his terrible deeds, the enemy shall utterly defile the sanctuary of God*." (Proclaim to be God, as in II Thessalonians 2:4)*

Since we have confirmed the date of the Abraham Accords treaty we are dealing with seven years of time which the Bible states clearly is the last seven years prior to the return of Jesus

Christ. The seventh year is equal to the seventh trumpet. Does anyone really believe that mortal man can make peace in the Middle East? What will bring peace to the Middle East? It will not be by the efforts of mortal man. This seven year treaty will be the road that leads to the magnificent return of the Lord of Lords and King of Kings. He alone will bring peace to the Nations

ISRAEL'S PROTECTION

Revelation 12:14 (KJV) "And to the woman were given two wings of a great eagle, that she might fly into the **wilderness**, into **her place**, where she is nourished for a time, times, and half a time, **from the face of the serpent**."

I've heard many stories about the Jews, that they will be leaving for Petra or they will be flown somewhere to safety. Stop and think about that it would be impossible for a million Jews let alone six million Jews to flee to safety, especially to Petra it will not happen that way, remember, they had to drag the Jews from Gaza several years ago. The protector for Israel is the second largest Air Force in the world, second only to the U.S.A and God is their ultimate protector.

Several years ago, my friend Terry brought an article to church that he downloaded from the Internet. Terry would constantly give me articles of interest that had something to do with Israel. I looked at the article, read it, and was amazed to find something that hit me right away. 102 brand new F16I fighter-bombers were given to Israel as a military grant from the USA. Well, I thought that was big news, as this information had been out for a couple of months but I never saw any of it in the papers or on the news! Hmm! It's hard to believe a $4.5 billion dollar deal, and it was low key in the papers!

Revelation 12:14[14] And to the woman were given two wings of a great eagle, that she might fly into the wilderness *(Negev desert),* into *(an air base built by America)* her place, *(where she is nourished for a time, and times, and half a time, her place),* from the face of the serpent.

Well I read on and was astounded to see that these planes were going to be located at an airbase in the Negev desert. "Wilderness" (the air base was built by the USA) "And that would be located in Israel (**her place**) and would protect Israel for the last 3½ years" and these planes would be located away from the 10-horned beast that will have a presence in Jerusalem *(Daniel 11:31)* for the last 3½ years, **away from the face of the serpent**. Every word fit. We both thought *"WOW"* how remarkable is God's' word. Their now getting F35 stealth from us.

As of this published 3rd edition and by way of our fraud government the scriptures are very clear Israel stands alone and even our fraud government is against Israel. I am hoping this fraud government will be removed and replaced. I see these events will need a strong leader at the time of this war and Biden is not the one.

Chapter 13:
Rapture of The Church

Why on earth would anyone believe that they are going to be raptured prior to the greatest witnessing season ever? God will use this season to multiply His kingdom, people rationalize, since they can't find the church after the fourth chapter of Revelation, The church must be gone, look at Revelation 4:1. After this I looked and there before me was a door standing open in heaven and the voice I had first heard speaking to me like a trumpet said, Come up here, and I will show you what must take place after this."

Jesus is telling the writer of Revelation, John, to come up and see what is going to happen in the future. Jesus will reveal it to him. It implies that the reason is so that John can finish writing about amazing things yet to come. Remember, Jesus instructed John to "Write down what you have just seen, and what will soon be shown to you" in Revelation 1:19 (RSB). For those of you who believe that Revelation Chapter four is the rapture, tell me, where are the harvesters and the angels spoken of in Matthew 24:31? Where is the trumpet call? Why doesn't Jesus address the Church? Why doesn't He summon the Church upward? Clearly, Jesus was speaking to John and him alone. The Church has not yet been raptured in Revelation 4:1. The Church is still on earth. We shouldn't overlook; Revelation 14:8, 9 and12 [8] And another angel followed, saying, "Babylon is fallen, is fallen, that great city, because she has made all nations drink of the wine of the wrath of her fornication."[9]

Then a third angel followed them, saying with a loud <u>voice</u>, "If anyone worships the beast and <u>his</u> image, and receives *his* mark on his forehead or on his <u>hand</u>,

[12] Here is the patience of the saints; here *are* those who keep the commandments of God and the faith of Jesus.

<u>Revelation 20:4</u> (KJV) "And I saw thrones, and they sat upon them, and judgment was given unto them: and I saw the souls of them that were beheaded for the witness of Jesus, and for the Word of God, and <u>which had not worshiped the beast, neither his image, neither had received his mark upon their foreheads, or in their hands;</u> and they lived and reigned with Christ for a thousand years."

See; Matthew <u>24:28-31</u>

<u>Revelation 20:5</u> (KJV) "But the rest of the dead lived not again until the thousand years were finished. This is the first resurrection."

<u>Revelation 20:6</u> (KJV) "Blessed and holy is he that has part in The First Resurrection on such the second death hath no power, but they shall be priests of God and of Christ, and shall reign with Him a thousand years."

If the Church was raptured in chapter four as others say, then who is left to be "beheaded for the witness of Jesus?" Why should Christians be concerned about receiving the mark of the beast? Who is the Lord warning about the mark? The answer is the church! The church remains on earth through the great tribulation. <u>Those who have not worshiped the beast, nor received his mark </u>will rule and reign with Christ for a thousand years.

The beast is in power prior to the rapture. Christians do not give their loyalty to the anti-Christ by accepting his mark. The ungodly do. The Lord rewards those that remain loyal to Him! What is His reward? ***Verse five of Revelation 20 states this is the "first resurrection"***! His reward is the rapture and the blessing of ruling and reigning with Christ for a thousand years from the New Jerusalem. You must remember this passage was written after Jesus was raised from the dead. It is not referring to His resurrection. The first resurrection spoken of in this verse is the rapture of the church! The Bible is correct; there can be no pre-tribulation rapture!

Look at Revelation 13:5-**7** (KJV) "And there was given unto him a mouth speaking great things and blasphemies; <u>and power was given unto him to continue for forty and two months</u>." He opened his mouth to blaspheme God, and to slander His name and His dwelling place and those who live in heaven. <u>He was given power to make war against the saints and to conquer them</u>. The anti-Christ can't wage war against the saints if they've already been raptured.

Why would anyone want to be raptured prior to the work being completed? When Jesus came to earth He was on a mission and He did not leave until His work was completed. We are to do the work of the Lord until He returns to receive us. I for one do not want to leave prior to the work being completed. I want to be the very last one raptured, how about you?

The more I study, the more I learn. I am just in shock, in awe, and completely taken back by what is penned. Take for example the mystery of God's words to Daniel to seal up the book until the time of the end. What the Lord has shown me has simply blown my mind. It's a mixture of sweet and sour. I praise the Lord for showing me what He has led me to receive. Sometimes I am dumbfounded, bewildered, amazed, upset, and in disbelief. My mind is staggered by what I have read and been able through His perfect word to piece together. I cannot comprehend the mind of God.

The devil has been given power to make war with the saints. Why? To prove us worthy to rule and reign with Christ.

The rapture is at the 7th trump or 7th year of the last 7 years.

1 Corinthians 15:52King James Version (KJV)

52 In a moment, in the twinkling of an eye, at the last trump: for the trumpet shall sound, and the dead shall be raised incorruptible, and we shall be changed.

PRAISE THE LORD!

Chapter 14:
There Shall Be A Time of
Trouble Such as Never Was!

Why should I know the information in this book?

I believe from what I've studied and garnered from pastors, theologians and prophecy gurus, most believe they will not be here when the great tribulation starts. Meaning they believe they will be raptured or removed from earth prior to this rapture event. They have not completed their homework and you as a member of a church have not taken the time to find out if they were right or wrong. Most of these pastors have just gone along with the false teaching of the past and a pretribulation rapture without really checking the facts. Why does it make a difference that they and we should know the truth. If you don't know and can't see the truth there is a point perhaps when morality will get so bad you will be deceived to believe the devils lies. This is what the bible alludes to, you will be deceived unless you are wearing the full armor of God. 2 Thessalonians 2:10-11, I will send a strong delusion that you will believe the lie.

Let's look at the facts of what is happening in the world today.

Our life's viewpoint is changing from mostly normal, to beheadings, killings, rapes, rampant crime actually anything that is drastically changing the way we live from better to worse. And abortion the slaughter of babies is incomprehensible.

There was a series of videos that portrayed a ho-hum attitude on how we live our lives and has told millions they will be raptured prior to any mass problems the bible has alluded to. They have portrayed an easy road for Christians, this is misinformation and very unfortunate. Jesus said, what they have done to me they will also do this to you. Most believe they will not go through any tribulation. Some Pentecostals even believe this, most all Baptists believe they will be gone prior. Let's just look at what has been unleashed upon the world, the following is a brief summary of what you will find in Revelation chapter 6.

THE WORLD AND ISLAM

If Europe had read and paid attention to their bibles they could have prevented the tragedy now taking place in Europe. America is next and is now in Islam's crosshairs.

This is an in your face bible prophecy written some 2000 years ago and no one is saying a word! This is proof of the accuracy of the bible and a great witnessing tool.

An event in human history as worthy of knowing as the parting of the Red sea for the Hebrews to cross over is happening before your eyes and no one is even mentioning it! WHY?

Allowing Muslims to migrate anywhere other than a Muslim country is a big mistake. Most people do not read the bible so here is what you need to know about Muslims and Islam.

Most people are not aware of what is taking place historically with the Muslim migration. If you would go to KJV Revelation 6 and read the whole chapter you will find these highlights. KJV Revelation 6:8 And I looked, and behold a PALE HORSE: and his name that sat on him was DEATH, and HELL followed with him. And power was given unto "THEM" over the fourth part of the earth, to KILL with sword, and with hunger, and with death, and with the beasts of the earth.

9 And when he had opened the fifth seal, I saw under the altar the souls of them that were slain (beheaded) for the word of God, and for the testimony which they held:

Black horse = Capitalism, White horse = Catholicism, Red horse = Communism, PALE HORSE = ISLAM. I can't imagine a pastor not telling their congregations what is happening. Deafening silence is all you hear.

God placed these prophecies so that we would not be ignorant of the times we are living in. I am telling you this and perhaps you will open the door to further study of the scriptures that will impact your lives in these end of the age years. A past Muslim inspired President is one of "them" and was comfortable with bringing his satanic brothers into this country, but you, are you comfortable with subjecting your family to these savages? If we lock the door this madness may not come to America. The current President has opened the door to countless

Personally I wish no harm to come to my family or yours and will do whatever necessary to combat this. How about you?

If European's had read and paid attention to their bibles they could have closed the door to further migration of the satanic Muslims. Our past President is one of "them" and was comfortable with bringing his satanic brothers into this country, but you, are you comfortable with subjecting your family to these savages? If we lock the door this madness may not come to America.

If you think this Muslim problem is going away anytime soon you are sorely mistaken. This madness will continue until Jesus Christ returns for His church. The problem is Americans have not been subjected to this madness on any scale that is equal to what Europe is going through. Why does this have to happen? If you say nothing and do nothing thinking this will not affect you, guess again. For most this is not a problem as it hasn't caused a problem for them, it's always a problem for someone else. I could spend all day on this to no avail as most know what is happening. My advice is to be well grounded in the Christ. Be vigilant, be smart about what is happening around you and do all you can to stop the Muslim migration to America. They bring their devil worship to a Christian country and won't assimilate?

Revelation 6Amplified Bible (AMP)

The Fifth Seal—Martyrs

[9] When He (the Lamb) broke open the fifth seal, I saw underneath the altar the souls of those who had been slaughtered because of the word of God, and because of the testimony which they had maintained [out of loyalty to Christ].[10] They cried in a loud voice, saying, "O Lord, holy and true, how long now before You will sit in judgment and avenge our blood on those [unregenerate ones] who dwell on the earth?" [11] Then they were each given a white robe; and they were told to rest *and* wait quietly for a little while longer, until *the number of* their fellow servants and their brothers and sisters who were to be killed even as they had been, would be completed.

The Sixth Seal—Terror

[12] I looked when He (the Lamb) broke open the sixth seal, and there was a great earthquake; and the sun became black as [h]sackcloth [made] of hair, and the whole moon became like blood; [13] and the stars of the sky fell to the earth, like a fig tree shedding its late [summer] figs when shaken by a strong wind. [14] The sky was split [separated from the land] and rolled up like a scroll, and every mountain and island were dislodged *and* moved out of their places.[15] Then the kings of the earth and the great men and the [i]military commanders and the wealthy and the strong and everyone, [whether] slave or free, hid themselves in the caves and among the rocks of the mountains;[16] and they called to the mountains and the rocks, "Fall on us and hide us from the face of Him who sits on the

throne, and from the [righteous] wrath *and* indignation of the Lamb; [17] for the great day of their wrath *and* vengeance *and* retribution has come, and who is able to [face God and] stand [before the wrath of the Lamb]?"

What are the advantages of knowing these prophecies of the book of Daniel?

The largest advantage is knowing prior so you might have time to get your loved ones to church and ultimately salvation. It can take years to get someone interested in salvation. Now you have this advantage. Have a son? Have a daughter...

The next advantage could well be in the food industry, there could be a shortage and if so, are you prepared? Perhaps for you it would not be a problem but what about your kids? Are you somewhere where food is plentiful? Are you prepared for people trying to steal your food?

And what about location. If there is a nuclear war do you live in a large metropolitan city? If you know the day that war will take place are you better off leaving that city?

I'm sure there are a host of other possibilities here and you can add to this list.

I must say this as the only place you will find this as you will not find this mentioned in most churches. For those of you that know the rapture might be but a few weeks away and you have friends and family that are not prepared to go in the rapture you may want to leave a note for those loved ones.

What they must do now is make it through Gods wrath which will be for 57 ½ days from the rapture of the church to the "1335 day" or the date listed in chapter 12 the Time Table and the Incredible Sevens.

If you miss the rapture;

Daniel 12:12 AMPC

[12] Blessed, happy, fortunate, spiritually prosperous, *and* to be envied is he who waits expectantly *and* earnestly [who endures without wavering beyond the period of tribulation] and comes to the 1,335 days!

I REST MY CASE!

"You only get one chance at getting it right"

Get it right!

My final comments;

The Judgment of Babylon / The Fall of America

I have studied this information for the better part of 16 years and till now I didn't have all of the information necessary to disclose. This third edition has the dates to the events listed in Daniel 12 with the two missing sets of days, Revelation 11 and words for interpretation of Daniel chapter 8.

I must tell you that what is coming on America will need a very strong and mighty President. Biden would walk away after giving in to the opposition. I believe Trump is that man that can see us through to the rapture. We are going to lose New York City, Babylon in Revelation 14:6-13 and with our borders wide open I see an invitation for the enemy to walk in with a devise to complete this dastardly deed. By Gods already knows what is going to happen and wants us to know by His word. America was founded on Christian principles, but has lost those principles long ago. As the bible states this judgment is for fornication and that leads to many things, one of which is Abortion 63 million or more children have been slaughtered. In China the total is well over 350, million and judgment will come on China in this war. Iran is the instigator of this war and will be severely punished also. Again why NYC? The first abortion to birth law signed into law on January 22, 2019. If you again will look at Daniel 8:19 God is bringing this to an end just as it says.

God in His mercy is giving America 3.5 years to prepare for this judgment which has trickled down to less than 2.5 years as of this writing as we are in the last 6 years, the date for this event is in Daniel chapter 12. It is imperative that residence of New York city and surrounding areas make plans to move from that area by a certain date. God has given us the exact date when this judgment will come. GUARENTEED!

I have proven all the above by Gods word and His completion numbers in this book. Blessed to be a blessing. Roger King

These next 3 chapters are the most important in the book! You can know all 15 previous chapters but that knowledge will not get you into heaven.

Only a heartfelt repentance of sins and a relationship with Jesus Christ along with being baptized in the name of Jesus by complete submersion will prepare you for the coming kingdom.

Most Pentecostal churches have baptism facilities!

Please do not miss the greatest event in human history, be prepared and fly away!

Chapter 15:
Baptism

I am placing this information in this book as many people believe that baptism is not a serious event. I disagree! I believe you must have the name of Jesus, the most powerful name in history imprinted in you as well as on you. Father, son and holy ghost are mere titles, you need the real name planted on you through baptism. This Jesus is responsible for your being. Father, son and holy ghost are not your savior Jesus is.

The following pages have all of the scriptures on Baptism that are in the bible and when viewed all together make it much easier to understand the meaning and reason for baptizing. A doctrine has arisen and is espoused by many churches that say baptism is not necessary for salvation, but it is simply an outward manifestation of an inward change. They say that grace plus nothing equals salvation. The Bible clearly says otherwise.

Nicodemus was questioning Jesus about baptism and Jesus answered him in John 3:3-5 Jesus answered and said unto him, "Verily, Verily, I say unto thee, except a man be born again, he cannot see the kingdom of God." Nicodemus saith unto him, "How can a man be born when he is old? Can he enter the second time into his mother's womb, and be born?" Jesus answered, "Verily, Verily, I say unto thee, except a man be born of water and of the spirit, he cannot enter into the kingdom of God."

The Bible does say we are saved by grace, but that doesn't mean all we have to do is say to ourselves that we believe and ask Jesus into our hearts, and we are saved. By His grace He gave us a way to be saved.

Titus 3:5 "Not by works of righteousness which we have done, but according to His mercy He saved us, by the washing of regeneration, and renewing of the Holy Ghost."

The saving of Noah and his family in the Old Testament was a type and shadow for those of us in the New Testament era to be saved, if we obey God, just as Noah obeyed God. It says that Noah was saved by water, and we are saved by water (baptism).

I Peter 3:20-21 "when once the long-suffering of God waited in the days of Noah, while the ark was a preparing, wherein few, that is, eight souls were saved by water, the like figure where unto even baptism doth also now save us by the resurrection of Jesus Christ."

Mark 16:16 "He that believeth and is baptized shall be saved; but he that believeth not shall be damned."

Many people key on the second part of this Scripture and say that since it does not mention baptism, baptism is not essential for salvation. However that first clause of this verse clearly says that you have to be baptized to be saved. The second clause simply means that if you don't believe, it doesn't matter what else you do, you will not be saved. The Bible says that we must obey the gospel, or we will be damned.

II Thessalonians 1: 7-9 "And to you who are troubled rest with us, when the Lord Jesus shall be revealed from heaven with his mighty angels. In flaming fire taking vengeance on them that know not God, and that obey not the gospel of our Lord Jesus Christ: Who shall be punished with everlasting destruction from the presence of the Lord, and from the glory of his power."

I Peter 4: 17 "For the time is come that judgment must begin at the house of God: and if it first begin at us, what shall the end be of them that obey not the gospel of God?"

What is the gospel? I Corinthians 15: 1-4 "Moreover, brethren, I declare unto you the gospel which I preached unto you, which also ye have received, and wherein ye stand; By which also ye are saved, if ye keep in memory what I preached unto you, unless ye have believed in vain. For I delivered unto you first of all that which I also received, how that Christ died for our sins according to the scriptures; And that he was buried and that he rose again the third day according to the scriptures."

So Paul is saying that the gospel is the death, burial and resurrection of Christ. How can we obey the death, burial, and resurrection of Christ? We don't literally have to die, be buried and raised from the dead. Jesus did this for us, but we have to have a symbolic death, burial and resurrection. The symbolic death is dying to self, giving up our self-rule and bowing to the ruler ship of Jesus Christ, putting off of the old man (the old lifestyle) and putting on the new:

Ephesians 4: 22-24 "That ye put off concerning the former conversations the old man, which is corrupt according to the deceitful lusts; And be renewed in the spirit of your mind; And that ye put on the new man, which after God is created in righteousness and true holiness."

Colossians 3: 9-10 "Lie not one to another, seeing that ye have put off the old man with his deeds; And have put on the new man, which is renewed in knowledge after the image of him that created him."

The symbolic burial is baptism.

Romans 6: 4 "Therefore we are buried with Him by baptism."

Furthermore the baptism must be by immersion in order to be a burial. Every baptism of which we have Biblical record was by immersion. The book of Acts, which is the history of the early Church, has recorded baptisms, and they all say that they went down into the water or something similar. The symbolic resurrection for us is the in filling of the Holy Ghost, which is the new life that enables us to live as a Christian should.

Romans 8: 11 "But if the spirit of Him that raised up Jesus from the dead dwell in you, He that raised up Christ from the dead shall also quicken your mortal bodies by his Spirit that dwelleth in you."

Peter verified this teaching on the Day of Pentecost. We know that Peter had the keys to the kingdom, in other words, the keys to salvation. Jesus was talking to Peter in <u>Matthew 16: 19</u> "And I will give unto thee the keys of the kingdom of heaven."

On the Day of Pentecost Peter was preaching to the people, telling them that the Jesus whom they had crucified was the Christ. The Bible says they were pricked in their hearts and asked what they should do? They had been waiting for the Messiah, but had missed him. Now they wanted to know what they should do to be saved.

Peter answered in: <u>Acts 2: 38-39</u> "Then Peter said unto them, Repent and be baptized every one of you in the name of Jesus Christ for the remission of sins, and ye shall receive the gift of the Holy Ghost. For the promise is unto you and to your children, and to all that are afar off even as many as the Lord our God shall call."

Here Peter has just given the plan of salvation: repent (death), be baptized in the name of Jesus (burial), and you shall receive the gift of the Holy Ghost (resurrection). Many people try to say that was for them in their time, but not for us now. However, we are still in the same dispensation as they were and verse 39 in Acts clearly states that this is not just for them and their children, but to all that are afar off, meaning us. Peter was clearly explaining how to be born again. When you are born again, you become part of the Kingdom of Jesus Christ.

IS IT WORTH TAKING THE CHANCE?

<u>Comments:</u> To anyone who has "not" been baptized in Jesus Name, I would like to say this. The Bible is very clear on this point. If you think you can just make it through the pearly gates being baptized in the name of the father, son and Holy Ghost take another look at Scripture.

It's very clear that you are to be baptized in the "NAME" of the Father, Son and Holy Ghost. <u>Who is the father, son, and Holy Ghost? **"JESUS"**</u>

Chapter 16:
The Oneness of God

There are many who say that Jesus is just one person in three-person Godhead, but the Bible tells us differently. It is a mystery and many miss it. Satan hates the truth, which is, there is one God who is above all. The Catholic Church made as part of their doctrine in the fourth century the idea that God is three persons: Father, Son, Holy Ghost and that Jesus is one of those three persons. This would suggest that Jesus resides in the Godhead. However, the Bible says otherwise.

Colossians 2: 8-9 "Beware lest any man spoil you through philosophy and vain deceit after the tradition of men, after the rudiments of the world, and not after Christ. For in Him (Jesus Christ) dwelleth all the fullness of the Godhead bodily." In other words, the Godhead (Father, Son, and Holy Ghost) resides in Jesus, rather than Jesus residing in the Godhead. The name of the Father is Jesus; the name of the Son is Jesus. The name of the Holy Ghost is Jesus. It's one God with more than one title, not three different persons. God's name was Jesus before he inhabited the body here on earth. In the Old Testament God manifested himself as an angel. In the New Testament, he manifested himself as a man. In the Old Testament His name was secret, to be revealed at Bethlehem. God revealed himself to Samson's father as an angel.

Judges 13: 16-18 "And the angel of the Lord said unto Manoah, "Though thou detain me, I will not eat of thy bread;

and if thou wilt offer a burnt offering, thou must offer it unto the Lord." For Manoah knew not that he was an angel of the Lord. "And Manoah said unto the angel of the Lord, "What is thy name, that when thy sayings come to pass we may do thee honour?"

"And the angel of the Lord said unto him, "Why askest thou thus after my name, seeing it is secret?" Jacob, too, asked God his name as he wrestled with him.

Genesis 32: 24-30 "And Jacob was left alone; and there wrestled a man with him until breaking of the day. And when he saw that he prevailed not against him, he touched the hollow of his thigh; and the hollow of Jacob's thigh was out of joint, as he wrestled with him. And he said, let me go, for the day breaketh. And he said, I will not let thee go except thou bless me. And he said unto him, what is thy name? And he said Jacob. And he said Thy name shall be called no more Jacob, but Israel: for as a prince hast thou power with God and with men, and hast prevailed. And Jacob asked him, and said Tell me, I pray thee, thy name. And he said, wherefore is it that thou dost ask after my name? And he blessed him there. And Jacob called the name of the place Penuel: for I have seen God face to face, and my life is preserved."

In Isaiah we are told that the Son is also the Father when the birth of Jesus is foretold.

Isaiah 9: 6 "For unto us a child is born, unto us a son is given; and the government shall be upon his shoulder; and his name shall be called Wonderful, Counselor, The Mighty God, The Everlasting Father and The Prince of Peace."

The first mention of God's name was in the New Testament: Matthew 1: 21 "And she shall bring forth a son, and thou shalt call his name JESUS: for he shall save his people from their sins."

How could he have a people already before he was born? Only if he was God Almighty.

Matthew 1: 23 "Behold, a virgin shall be with child, and shall bring forth a son, and they shall call his name Emmanuel, which being interpreted is, God with us."

The Bible also says he declared his Father's name. John 5: 43 "I am come in my Father's name, and ye received me not: if another shall come in his own name, him ye will receive."

What name did he come in? Jesus. So Jesus is the Father's name.

In the New Testament Jesus told the Jews that he had seen Abraham, as though he were around in Abraham's day: John 8: 56-58 "Your father Abraham rejoiced to see my day: and he saw it, and was glad. Then said the Jews unto him, Thou art not yet fifty years old and hast thou seen Abraham? Jesus said unto them, Verily, Verily I say unto you, Before Abraham was, I am."

When the Bible speaks of the right hand of God, it means the place of authority.

Matthew 28: 18 "And Jesus came and spake unto them, saying, "All power is given unto me in heaven and in earth."

If Jesus has it all, there is none left for the other two, if there are three. Isaiah 43: 10-11 "Ye are my witnesses," saith the Lord, "and my servant whom I have chosen: that ye may know and believe me, and understand that I am he: before me there was no God formed, neither shall there be after me. I, even I, am the Lord; and beside me there is no Saviour."

This is before Jesus ever came to the earth. The God of the Old Testament is saying that he is the Savior, and we know that the Savior is Jesus. There are places in the Bible that say that Jesus is the Father, that Jesus is the Holy Ghost, that the Holy Ghost is the Father. There are not three separate persons, only one.

Jesus is the Father: When Philip asked Jesus to show them the Father, Jesus answered:

John 14: 9 "Jesus saith unto him, Have I been so long time with you, and yet hast thou not knownme, Philip? He that hath seen me hath seen the Father, and how sayest thou then, Shew us the Father?"

Holy Ghost is the Father: Matthew 1: 18 "Now the birth of Jesus Christ was on this wise: When as his mother Mary was espoused to Joseph, before they came together, she was found with child of the Holy Ghost."

Jesus is the Holy Ghost: <u>John 14: 17-18</u> "Even the Spirit of truth; whom the world cannot receive, because it seeth him not neither knoweth him: but ye know him; for he dwelleth with you, and shall be in you. I will not leave you comfortless: I will come to you."

Jesus is talking about the Holy Spirit coming to us for a comfort, but he is also saying that He will come to us. He is the Holy Spirit.

We are told that Godliness is a mystery, but it is revealed to us in the New Testament:

<u>I Timothy 3:16</u> "And without controversy great is the mystery of godliness: God was manifest in the flesh, justified in the Spirit, seen of angels, preached unto the Gentiles, believed on in the world, received up into glory."

This passage is talking about Jesus Christ. He was not the second person of the trinity. In order for God to reveal himself, he had to have a body. This was revealed to us because God knew that a false doctrine would emerge. Back to Colossians 2: 8-9, we are warned: "Beware lest any man spoil you through philosophy and vain deceit, after the tradition of men, after the rudiments of the world, and not after Christ. For in him dwelleth all the fullness of the Godhead bodily."

Who was Paul warning here? To whom was Paul writing? He was writing to the believers, to The Church, to those who were born again. He was not writing to the unbelievers. Those who are not born again can believe and do whatever they want;

they are not going to heaven anyway. Paul was warning against false doctrine, which did emerge. The Catholic Church embraced the idea of the trinity around 325 A.D. Many of The Churches that broke away from the Catholic Church because of doctrinal differences still embraced the idea of the trinity.

Deuteronomy 6: 4 "Hear, O Israel: The Lord our God is one Lord."

Satan could not overcome the power of Christ, but he could pervert the doctrine: trinity.

He could not overcome baptism, but he could change the form. There is no power in "Father." The power is in the name. There is no power in "Son." The power is in the name. There is no power in "Holy Ghost." The power is in the name: Jesus Christ. When the Catholic Church took the name out of baptism, they took the power out of baptism. When Jesus told the disciples to "teach all nations baptizing them in the name of the Father, and of the Son, and of the Holy Ghost." The disciples understood that the name (singular) is Jesus. Baptizing with the phrase "in the name of the Father, and of the Son, and of the Holy Ghost" is just the recipe. You have to put the ingredient in. That is just what they did in the early church: they baptized in the name of Jesus because Jesus is the name of the Father, Son and Holy Ghost.

God's name was kept secret in the Old Testament so that when he showed up; Satan would not know who he was and blow the plan of salvation. In Matthew 24, Jesus said that "many false prophets shall rise, and shall deceive many. And because iniquity shall abound, the love of many shall wax cold. But he that shall endure unto the end, the same shall be saved." The Mystery of Godliness was a mystery on purpose. The prophecy of Isaiah was fulfilled. They have ears to hear, but do not hear, eyes to see, but do not see. Jesus taught in parables to veil the truth to some, reveal the truth to others. Those who are not searching for the truth will not find it.

If you were baptized in the name of the Father Son and Holy Ghost I strongly urge you to get re-baptized in the name of Jesus. I have given out this advice before only to be told that they were baptized once and they're not doing it again. Well even pastors make mistakes but your salvation is of your own making. The devil will tell you anything, it's your responsibility to read the Bible and proceed accordingly. You are supposed to know the truth yourself. From all the books I've read on ancient writings I cannot believe anyone would want to go to hell or not do all in his power to keep that from happening. I strongly urge you to repent of your sins and get re-baptized.

There is one and only one God, and Jesus is that God.

Chapter 17:
The New Jerusalem

There is a need to place this chapter as many people cannot fathom a city this big or even where it will be located. I have placed all the scriptures I can find on this city so you can see at a glance what they say and mean. These verses will surprise you. There are no less than 17 verses that describe this city and remember every jot and tittles mean something. This is a constructed city, it has been built. This is not a chunk of dirt that blew out of some big explosion as the evolutionist would theorize. This has been constructed. If you have an opportunity to read my book THE WATCHERS, (who watches us from the moon and where did the fallen angles go?) you will find the moon is hollow and was constructed also. Where will the saints live? There are no words to describe the New Jerusalem except what the Bible says. It's unimaginable to say the least.

In John 14:2 - 3 Jesus states: "In my father's house are many mansions; if it were not so, I would have told you. I go to prepare a place for you. "And if I go to prepare a place for you, I will come again and receive you onto my self; that where I am you may be also."(That where I am, you may be also: where He lives, we will also live. He is going to bring His father's house of many mansions with Him.) In Revelation 20:4 Jesus said we would rule and reign with Him for 1000 years. In Revelation 3:12 Jesus states: "He who overcomes, I will make him a pillar in the temple of my God, and he shall go out no more. And I will write on him the name of MY GOD and the name of the city of MY GOD, the New Jerusalem, **which comes down out of heaven from my God.**

In <u>Revelation 21:2-3</u> John states: "Then I, John, saw the holy city, New Jerusalem, coming down out of heaven from God,

prepared as a bride adorned for her husband." (Coming down out of, clearly states where it's coming from.) 3 "And I heard a loud voice from heaven saying, Behold, the tabernacle of God is with men, and He will dwell with them, and they shall be His people, and God Himself will be with them and be their God." (Tabernacle of God, Its Gods' city, it's where God lives.)

<u>Revelation 21:12</u> "Also she had a great and high wall with twelve gates, and twelve angels at the gates, and names written on them, which are the names of the twelve tribes of the children of Israel."(The dictionary states that she means, <u>the object or thing before named or understood</u>, personified as a boat or the moon or the New Jerusalem that will be almost as big as the moon.)

<u>Revelation 21:16-18</u> "and the city was laid out as a square, and its length is as great as its breadth. And he measured the city with the reed: twelve thousand furlongs its length, breadth, and height are equal. (This is a city, the city of God. 12,000 furlongs divided by eight equals 1500 miles) 17 "Then he measured its wall; one hundred and forty and four cubits, according to the measurement of a man, this of an angel. (This is the thickness of the walls, 144 cubits or 216 feet. Cubits

times 1.5 equal feet) 18 "And the <u>construction</u> of the walls was of pure Jasper; and the city was pure gold, like clear glass. (According to the dictionary, construction means, the act of construction, also, that which is constructed. <u>I go to prepare a place!</u>)

<u>Revelation 21:19-24</u> "And the foundations of the wall of the city were adorned with all kinds of precious stones": Jasper which is clear as crystal; Sapphire which is blue, pale blue, with a star effect; Chalcedony which is milky, whitish, bluish gray, greenish, yellowish; Emerald which is light green to deep green; Sardonyx, a variety of onyx, light-colored chalcedony and reddish carnelian; Sardius, a stone in the breast plate of the Hebrew High Priest; Chrysolyte, old gold, yellow gold tending to tarnish; Beryl, all the above and below; Topaz, translucent, yellow gold, honey yellow, rarely blue green pink or red; Chrysoprasus, apple green with white and gray streaks; Jacinth, orange red, dark red, red light red, violet red; Amethyst, transparent all shades of violet. 22 "And I saw no temple therein: for the Lord God Almighty and the Lamb are the temple of it." (IT = Singular object) 23 And the city had no need of the sun, neither of the moon, to shine in it: for the glory of God did lighten it, and the Lamb is the light thereof. 24 "And the nations of them which are saved shall walk in the light of it: and the Kings of the earth do bring their glory and honor into it." (<u>Into it:</u> Inside and everyone on earth shall see its light in Verse 23 for the glory of God illuminated it, and the Lamb is its light. If you walk in its light, you must walk under it.)

Revelation 21:27 "And there shall in no wise <u>enter into it</u> anything that defileth, neither whatsoever worketh an abomination, or maketh a lie: but they which are written in the Lamb's book of life." (<u>Enter it:</u> once again we see those words and if your name is in the Lambs book of life you will be there, very clear.)

Revelation 22:3 "And there shall be no more curse: but the throne of God and of the Lamb shall be in it; and his servants shall serve Him.

Revelation 22:12: "And behold, I come quickly; and my reward is with me, to give every man according as his work shall be."

Isaiah 40:10 "Behold, the Lord God will come with strong hand, and his arm shall rule for him: behold, his reward is with him, <u>and his work before him</u>."

Isaiah 62:11 "Behold, the Lord has proclaimed unto the end of the world, Say ye to the daughter of Zion, Behold, thy salvation cometh; behold, his reward is with him, <u>and his work before him</u>.

And I will write on him my name This is an acknowledgement that in baptism the name of **"Jesus"** will be on you. Father, Son or the Holy Ghost are only titles.

THE NEW JERUSALEM STATISTICS

The moon is 2,080 miles in diameter. The New Jerusalem is 1,500 miles all ways, to form a cube and if in an orbit around the earth at about the same height as the moon would probably look about the same size as it is a cube.

The square miles of the first floor = 2,250,000

The cubic Miles = 3,375,000,000

The total height in feet = 7,920,000

If there were a floor, every 50' there would be 158,400 floors or 356,400,000,000 square miles of floor area. That should be enough for all the Saints to live.

Can you imagine everyone singing Majesty at the same time? 216' thick walls of Jasper. This would have to be the best sound box ever devised.

Total exterior surface = 13,500,000 sq. miles

Total cubic miles of Jasper in the exterior walls = 562,462.5

I know this stagers the mind that this could be constructed, but consider this, in my book "The Watchers", there is an article on the moon being an artificial hollow satellite of the earth, and that means it was constructed which has been proven to be true. I believe God can do anything as evidenced by making this fantastic universe and of course making us. What an awesome God!

Conclusion

By now you have read all the material in this book and realize that God left some big surprises for us all!

You have found that fornication/abortion is positively a no, no, and the price America and all citizens will pay is hard to imagine but He has spelled it out for us with the fall of New York City and the possible exodus of 8m people. You now know there **"is" big time judgment** and in case you are still not saved there is hell to follow unless you repent of your sins and are baptized in Jesus name. He has made you aware of the date of His return And to make sure you are aware, **there is no second chance**, as mentioned in the book you are in the last 7 years and if you are called by God to the alter and do not go it may be your last possible opportunity to obtain salvation. You will find this prophecy in 2 Thessalonians 2:10-11.

I haven't a clue as to how many of us will make it through to the rapture but if I make it through I am hoping to see all Christians at church on the night of His arrival outside weather permitting with as many search lights pointed skyward as possible.

I believe we need to give Jesus a welcome only He deserves. There is no one like Him. He has accepted us and kept us from the pits of hell. Thank you Jesus.

This prophecy on the war and return was extremely large and I knew I could never personally get all of this information out by voice nor can all of it be understood without it being printed so it can be read several times. I pray that I unraveled the scriptures enough for you to completely understand this prophecy. I have spent 16 years working on this as I could as the information came. You have no idea how amazed I am at what God can let you see and know, and how He can direct your path to the accomplishment of the greatest work of your lifetime. I praise you Lord and I thank Him for allowing me to accomplish this work and message.

There is no way in words I can tell you how it feels to have been able to accomplish this great task. Every day working on this was a blessing beyond blessings. For 16 years **no one** would believe this or what I said regarding my findings save my close friends whom I believe were God sent in the event of my not being present to explain this. I sent out 4000 of my first books in 2006 to Pentecostal pastors to find someone greater than I to follow this through to the end but not one reply and it had the key to unlocking Daniel 12.

For any of you unbelievers "YES" God is the author of every word in the bible as it is written, there are no mistakes and the words were penned by humans just like you and me and the chapters were numbered by a painter at Gods direction as evidenced by America being first mentioned in Daniel Independence Day or 7:4.

I EXPECT TO SEE EVERY ONE THAT READS THIS IN HEAVEN!

Thanks for purchasing my book and don't forget if you haven't ordered my book, (THE WATCHERS) do so now. The Watchers or better known as the fallen angels will be back in the last 3.5 years. Yes, you can download it but it really is nice to have it with a nice shinny cover on it. You can also order The Watchers on line. Just go to: www.thewatcherslive.com

Church affiliations;

Life Tabernacle Church
1130 Middlebury St
Elkhart, In 46516
Mark Johnson Pastor
574 293 9332
20 year member.

The Sanctuary
1043 Lehman St
Osceola, In
8 year member
Jack Rorie pastor

End time ministries
Irvin Baxter Deceased